Next Level Screenwriting

Next Level Screenwriting is an intermediate screenwriting book, for those that have already learned the basics of screenwriting, written a screenplay or two and want to bring their writing and stories to the next level.

Each chapter of the book examines a specific aspect of screenwriting, such as character, dialogue and theme, and then provides the reader with ideas, tips and inspiration to apply to their own writing. Rather than being another "how to" book, this volume features a variety of case studies and challenging exercises throughout – derived from a broad selection of successful feature films and TV shows from the 1940s to the present day – to help spark the imagination of the writer as they work through different styles and approaches of screenwriting.

An absolute must-read for any screenwriter wanting to improve their writing and storytelling skills.

David Landau is an award-winning screenwriter and playwright with seven plays published and is the author of the books *Lighting for Cinematography* and *Film Noir Production* in addition to numerous articles on screenwriting for such magazines as *Script, Screenwriter's Monthly, Student Filmmakers Magazine* and *HD ProGuide*. His feature screenwriting credits include *Murder at Café Noir* and *Dark Tarot*. David earned his MFA in Screenwriting from Goddard College and is a full Professor at Fairleigh Dickinson University. He is also a member of the Dramatists Guild and the University Film & Video Association.

David Bennett Carren is an award-winning screenwriter whose work includes numerous episodes for such television shows as *Star Trek: The Next Generation, Stargate SG1, Martial Law, Dennis the Menace,* and *Teenage Mutant Ninja Turtles* among others. His feature films include *Mr. Hell* and *Waiting for Sandoval*, and he was the writer/director on the feature film *The Red Queen*. A member of the Writers Guild of America and the University Film & Video Association, David earned his MFA in Screenwriting from Spalding University and is an Associate Professor at the University of Texas Rio Grande Valley where he is the Interim Chair of the Department of Theatre.

Next Level Screenwriting

Insights, Ideas and Inspiration for the Intermediate Screenwriter

David Landau and David Bennett Carren

LONDON AND NEW YORK

First published 2019
by Routledge
2 Park Square, Milton Park, Abingdon, Oxon, OX14 4RN

and by Routledge
52 Vanderbilt Avenue, New York, NY 10017

Routledge is an imprint of the Taylor & Francis Group, an informa business

© 2019 David Landau and David Bennett Carren

The right of David Landau and David Bennett Carren to be identified as authors of this work has been asserted by them in accordance with sections 77 and 78 of the Copyright, Designs and Patents Act 1988.

All rights reserved. No part of this book may be reprinted or reproduced or utilised in any form or by any electronic, mechanical, or other means, now known or hereafter invented, including photocopying and recording, or in any information storage or retrieval system, without permission in writing from the publishers.

Trademark notice: Product or corporate names may be trademarks or registered trademarks, and are used only for identification and explanation without intent to infringe.

Library of Congress Cataloging-in-Publication Data
Names: Landau, David, 1956- author. | Carren, David Bennett, author.
Title: Next level screenwriting : insights, ideas and inspiration for the intermediate screenwriter / by David Landau and David Bennett Carren.
Description: New York : Routledge, Taylor & Francis Group, 2019. | Includes bibliographical references and index.
Identifiers: LCCN 2018057340| ISBN 9780367151515 (hardback) | ISBN 9780367151584 (paperback) | ISBN 9780429055386 (e-book)
Subjects: LCSH: Motion picture authorship.
Classification: LCC PN1996 .L28 2019 | DDC 808.2/3–dc23
LC record available at https://lccn.loc.gov/2018057340

ISBN: 978-0-367-15151-5 (hbk)
ISBN: 978-0-367-15158-4 (pbk)
ISBN: 978-0-429-05538-6 (ebk)

Typeset in Bembo
by Swales & Willis, Exeter, Devon, UK

From David Bennett Carren: I wish to dedicate this book to my colleagues, administration, and staff at the University of Texas Rio Grande Valley; talented, supportive and superlative people all. I also wish to thank my wife Marilyn and my children, Max and Savannah, for their infinite understanding and patience. But most of all I appreciate my co-author David Landau, who has made the experience of working on this project a total joy.

From David Landau: I would like to dedicate this book to my screenwriting students and their love of writing, to my children Tracey and Alexandra, and most of all my loving wife Wendy for all her support and encouragement.

We would both like to dedicate this book to all those that have the inspiration, drive and obsession with creative writing. Storytelling is one of the noblest professions.

Contents

Introduction   xi

1 Don't be afraid of genre   1
  Enjoying the genre 1
  Crossing genres 2
  Horror comedy 4
  Genre expectations and bending them 6
  A final note 9
  What did we learn? 9
  Exercise 9

2 The write approach   11
  Motivated style 12
  The internal approach 13
  Maintaining an established style 14
  Style that fits the genre 16
  What did we learn? 16
  Exercise 16

3 Character depth   18
  Motivating your characters 18
  Unmasking your characters 21
  Humor is character 23
  The other character change 24
  Television characters 27
  What did we learn? 29
  Exercise 30

4 Dialogue that does more than further the plot — 31
A distinct voice 32
Attitude dialogue 35
Period dialogue 37
Dialogue that reveals character 39
Poetic dialogue 41
Contemporary dialogue 43
When talk is action 46
What did we learn? 48
Exercise 48

5 Poetic description — 49
Choosing your words 49
Describing for the mind's eye 51
Writing for the reader 52
Humorously said 54
What did we learn? 55
Exercise 56

6 Finding the theme — 57
Popular movies have themes 57
Shared themes of westerns and horror 59
We have met the enemy and they are us 59
The stronger the theme, the stronger the story 60
Even comedy has a theme 61
The naked theme 62
What did we learn? 64
Exercise 65

7 First-person narrative screenwriting — 66
Narration that isn't a crutch 66
Hard-boiled witty narration 69
Found footage as first person 71
Mockumentary 73
What did we learn? 77
Exercise 77

8 Managing multiple-protagonist syndrome or ensembles — 78
Ensemble vs. episodic 78
Linking stories 79

Playing with time 80
Ensemble characters 81
Recurring locations 82
The ensemble anchor 83
Ensemble in the park 84
The trouble with ensemble 85
Ensemble in television 87
A note on television dialogue 91
What did we learn? 95
Exercise 95

9   Based on true events and research   97
Adapting history 97
Free yourself from the truth 99
Find a special event in history 102
Find a special place in history 103
Research that works for you 106
This all applies to television 108
This all applies to everything you write 108
What did we learn? 109
Exercise 109

10 Set-up, pay-off and the twist   110
The Twilight Zone set-up/pay-off 111
Twist ending set-up/pay-offs 112
Character, character, character 112
Twists in TV 115
Comedy set-up/pay-off 116
The Aristotle connection 116
What did we learn? 117
Exercise 117
Bonus exercise 118

11 Writing for a budget   119
Micro-budget feature 119
Independent low budget 121
Hollywood low budget 123
Limited-budget TV 124
What did we learn? 124
Exercise 125

12	**Rewriting: The pain and the gain**	126
	Working in backstory 128	
	The development rewrite 129	
	The production rewrite 131	
	The post-production rewrite 133	
	A note on taking notes 133	
	Three tricks to taking notes 134	
	What did we learn? 135	
	Exercise 135	
13	**Wrote the script, now what?**	136
	Copyright 137	
	Feedback 137	
	Contests 139	
	Producers and agents 140	
	They call it Hollywood 142	
	Pitching 143	
	How hard is pitching? 144	
	Goodbye Hollywood 144	
	Make it yourself 145	
	Low-budget independents 146	
	How and how much? 146	
	Show me the money – in the movies 146	
	Show me the money – in television 147	
	Don't undo your sale 148	
	What did we learn? 148	
	Exercise 149	
	Index	151

Introduction

This book is meant for people who have already read a screenwriting book or two, taken a screenwriting class, or written a screenplay or two. It isn't another "how to write your first screenplay" book, but rather a "how to do more with your writing" book. We, the authors, thought of it more as a "Screenwriting II" book. Of course, we certainly hope that the material in this book will be of interest to a writer at any level of screenwriting, from beginner to intermediate to more experienced.

David Carren and I have both taught beginning and advanced screenwriting college courses for many years. While there is a plethora of books we can chose from for our Screenwriting I classes, finding a book for Screenwriting II has been a challenge we have often lamented over at University Film & Video Association Conferences (yeah, a couple of hundred film/video professors spend a week together geeking out over film stuff once a year). Over our iced teas, we complained that since our Screenwriting II students have already learned about most of the concepts written in any fine screenwriting book, (three-act structure; the hero's journey; character arc; protagonist goal; antagonist motivation; kinds of conflict; uses of dialogue; professional screenplay format; condensing description; etc.) what book could we use for the next level or advanced screenwriting course that didn't spend most of its pages repeating them?

There's always so much more to cover and talk about after the basics, but there's not enough room to go into that in even the best "how to write a screenplay" book. And reviewing concepts in a new light is also a very helpful thing. So, what do we use? There are a few good books that concentrate on dialogue and a few good ones that are about the rewriting process, which are great subjects. But we want to help our students grow as writers by giving them examples that excite and inspire, that give them new ideas and help them explore more advanced concepts within screenwriting and remind them of valuable basics. So, one summer, I said to David, "Maybe we should write an intermediate screenwriting book – you know, something that might inspire our students to take their writing to the next level."

We put our pens where our mouths were and wrote this book. We wanted to address some more advanced concepts within screenwriting, such as ensemble storytelling, successful use of narration, research, advanced description writing, rewriting, and a little about the business of screenwriting – basically, the stuff we cover in more advanced level screenwriting classes, deliberately avoiding most of the things that are covered in beginning screenwriting courses and books. Each chapter of this book looks at a variety of successful screenplays from feature films and dramatic TV from which any writer can gain some insight. They range from classics to modern streaming shows. But they all serve as examples as to how some writers achieved certain creative concepts or addressed certain creative goals.

This book doesn't really have to be read in any order, although we did break it down into 13 chapters so that it could be used as a text in a standard advanced screenwriting class (which is 15 weeks, allowing one week off for mid-term and one off for final). At the end of each chapter we added writing exercises, for those that feel like a challenge.

Warning: You won't find in this text discussions on such things as screenplay format, three-act structure, plot points, forms of conflict, false climax, hero's journey, subplot, moment of loss, and other basic important screenwriting concepts. Other books cover these things very nicely and thoroughly, and we hope you've already read one or two of them before coming to our book.

We are always growing as writers and artists. We can learn a lot from those that came before us. Painters study the masters, novelists study the classics. Screenwriters have a huge body of wonderful works that we can read and gain insight, ideas, tips and inspiration from. We hope that this book will provide you, the reader, with just that and help you bring your writing and stories to the next level.

– David Landau

1 Don't be afraid of genre

Enjoying the genre

The reality is that many people often select the movie they want to watch based on its apparent genre. What do they feel like seeing tonight? What sounds like fun? Or, more important, how does this film offer something expected yet also fresh and new within the strictures of its genre? Genre is a promise that writers and filmmakers make to the audience. Genres provide viewers with certain expectations based on the perceived nature of the film they came to see. No one wants to see a romantic comedy that ends with a tragic, violent death or a horror film that ends with "it was all a joke." It is unfortunate that some young writers and writing tutors seem to turn their noses up at the very idea of writing within a genre, particularly the most popular or mainstream examples. The truth is, these supposedly despised or disrespected categories of film are usually what the audience wants, but this doesn't mean we writers have to be clichéd or unoriginal. What a writer does within the genre can be fresh and original. To accomplish this a writer needs to be respectful of the conceits of the genre, and of the audience that wants to enjoy it.

However a writer approaches their story, whatever tale they may be trying to tell, it can, will, or should be defined by a genre of some kind. The more thought, study or knowledge the writer gives to the genre they are working in, the better equipped they will be to understand and develop their own story. This will be the case even if the writer intends to bend, twist, or break that genre in some startling or interesting way. Bottom line: know your genre, whether or not you intend to completely reinvent it.

In any case, no one has to write a mainstream genre story, but its creation can be a lot of fun and very rewarding. Whether it's westerns, horror, war, romantic comedy, musicals, spy stories, or some cross mixture of all of the above, they all contain certain elements that the audience expects, and the writer is obligated to provide. The use, timing and twists on these elements can make some genre scripts and movies far more entertaining, popular and artistically rewarding than others.

Damien Chazelle did just that with his musical *La La Land* (2016.) He wrote a script that contained all the genre elements of the classic musical, but told them in an original, refreshing way and then diverted from the typical genre happy ending with a more bittersweet and touching resolution. But he still fulfilled all the audience's expectations, even going above and beyond. Boy meets girl, they struggle towards their dreams together, one succeeds while one suffers, they drift apart, they rescue and inspire each other – and then they're both happy in the end. Besides employing a unique structure in how he told his story, Damien's ending was totally original – the romantic couple finds happiness but not together. The film was an enormous box office success and earned six Academy Awards. It's a genre picture, but it's clear Damien had fun writing within the genre.

David Peoples' screenplay for *The Unforgiven* (1992) is a genre western. It has everything the audiences could expect to see in a western but with one singular exception – it reverses the paradigm of the fallen gunslinger finding redemption. In this film, the gunslinger, a tortured and guilt stricken individual who has reached an inner peace and forsworn violence, literally loses his soul and returns to violence by the end of the film. It was nominated for nine Academy Awards, won four and was a big box office hit.

Peter Chiarelli and Adele Lin's screenplay for *Crazy Rich Asians* (2018), based on the book by Kevin Kwan, is a genre romantic/comedy that finds a new take on Cinderella; one of the oldest stories ever told. Here, the unusual environment, characters and situation make the old new again, succeeding with both critics and audiences alike.

All of these films fulfilled the genre expectations the audience went to their movies to see, but also delivered something original and different within it. But even if a writer decided to approach a genre film in a traditional manner without attempting to reinvent the form in some way, this wouldn't be a cop out. Working in any recognizable genre is not as simple or easy as others would have one believe. To craft a good genre piece, the writer needs to be fully aware of its expectations, elements and trappings. Even before they begin, they need to have watched and analyzed many years of that genre's pictures. What do they all have in common? What are their recurring plot points? What are their character arcs? What are their typical act breaks? What did critics and audiences appreciate the most? How did past writers stick to the genre structure but vary it and make it their own?

Most of all, any genre writer needs to actually enjoy the one they have chosen to work in as much as they enjoy watching and reading it. Only by understanding and respecting a genre can a writer change, adapt or break it.

Crossing genres

Crossing genres is endemic to the film industry now, not only in this country but across the world. For the last two decades, Luc Besson has been bringing a French sensibility and Gallic locales to American-style high-concept action, fantasy, and science fiction films like his *Taken, The Fifth Element, The Transporter,* and *Lucy,* often succeeding and sometimes even reinventing or expanding on the themes, intentions, and possibilities of these genres. However, even Luc Besson, with all his experience and resources, couldn't produce a success with one of his most ambitious projects, *Valerian and the City of a Thousand Planets* (2017), because his screenplay didn't contain intriguing protagonists with a truly involving or unexpected story.

The Chinese film industry has also made a strenuous attempt to break into the world (particularly the American) market with cross-genre projects like *The Great Wall* (2016), an uneasy mix of fantasy, horror, history, and romance, which also failed because of story and character problems. In particular, it's highly unwise in any fantasy, horror, historical romance to have the adventurer hero driving its plot, William Garen (Matt Damon), fall in love with a beautiful female Chinese soldier (Jing Tian) but have him ride away at the end of the movie with his male buddy, leaving her alone on the Great Wall! Sometimes, just a bad ending can defeat all the best efforts of an entire cross-genre screenplay.

While mixing genres is rife throughout film it's especially prevalent in television, which has entered a new Golden Age with literally hundreds of dramas being produced. But whether the genres being mixed are the carefully calibrated character and zombie drama displayed in *The Walking Dead,* character and crime drama of *Breaking Bad,* or the character and political drama of *House of Cards,* the foundations of these projects cannot function beyond the solid development of the people in their worlds, no matter how bizarre or over the top the worlds may be.

In *Jane the Virgin,* (2014–) an absolutely absurd premise, that a young virginal woman could be accidentally inseminated, is made believable, accessible and wildly entertaining through a deft mix of comedy, drama, and the distinct and unique components of a telenovela. In the pilot, written by Jennie Synder Urman, based on the Venezuelan soap opera *Juana La Virgen,* every scene is unexpected thanks to the angle from which it is approached, the characters' reactions, the use of voice-over, imagery, and graphics, or all of the above. A superb example is when the doctor who accidentally inseminated Jane confirms she's pregnant. The scene focuses on Jane's astonished response, the series narrator's voice-over, and the imaginary support of a fantasy telenovela character.

```
Jane is just staring at her, in shock. Time seems to slow. We are
PUSHING IN: on Jane as her heart beats. We become aware of the
sound. THUMP THUMP. THUMP THUMP. THUMP THUMP.

Jane looks down and is startled to see Rubio (the telenovela
star) kneeling in front of her! In subtitled Spanish:
```

> RUBIO
> It's alright. Just take deep
> Breaths... in and out. In and out.

Jane is a little confused, but starts breathing deeply.

> LATIN LOVER NARRATOR
> It is important to note that right
> now Jane is having an out of body
> experience. None of this is really
> happening.

> RUBIO
> (to Jane)
> I know exactly how you feel. When
> I found out that the deepest,
> truest love of my life, was really
> my half sister born as a result of
> my father's secret double life, I
> was devastated.

> LATIN LOVER NARRATOR
> (rapidly, dramatically)
> It seems that, unable to process
> the cosmic joke that had just
> happened to her, Jane's mind had
> jumped to the only other event that
> was even remotely as outrageous –

> RUBIO
> I got through that, Jane. And you
> will get through this.

Magical realism and character comedy has been successfully woven together to create something fresh, fun, and sincere. While this moment is amusing and unexpected, it's also accessible and true, even arguably realistic. If you just found out you had been accidentally inseminated, would your reaction be any less shocked or surreal?

Horror comedy

Returning to film, another superb example of a satisfying mix of genres is the zombie-drama-comedy *Shaun of the Dead* (2004), written by Simon Pegg and Edgar Wright. As in all successful cross-genre projects, this one gathers together a slew of seemingly incongruous and disparate elements then integrates them into a satisfying whole. While the story of Shaun, his friends and family journeying to a local London pub to take shelter against the flesh-hungry hordes of a zombie apocalypse is undeniably funny, it never neglects the elements of fear and suspense that support a proper undead horror film. Neither does it ever lose its focus on its characters, carefully establishing them as real people with realistic relationships and concerns.

For example, after Philip, Shaun's stepfather, is bitten, and near death, the man has a moment with his stepson where he addresses their fraught history in accessible, touching terms.

>   SHAUN
>   Philip, you don't have to
>   explain...
>
>   PHILIP
>   I do. I've always loved you Shaun,
>   always thought you had it in you to
>   do well. You just need motivation.
>   Somebody to prove yourself to. I
>   thought that could be me.
>
> SHAUN nods, eyes wide. With huge effort, PHILIP puts his hand on SHAUN's shoulder.
>
>   PHILIP (CONT'D)
>   Take care of your Mum, there's a
>   good boy.
>
> PHILIP slips away. SHAUN closes his dead step-dad's eyes.

These characters connect for perhaps the first and only time as a stepfather and son right before the poor man dies. This is a moment – identifiable, human, and engaging – that would provide strong emotional purchase for any drama. However, a few scenes later, as Philip transforms into a blood-thirsty zombie, and Shaun locks him in their car, we have a completely different moment. While a raucous piece of music the living Philip would have despised is playing on the car's radio, Shaun tries to reason with his distraught mother who is in denial about her undead husband.

>   BARBARA
>   I'm sure if we just –
>
>   SHAUN
>   That's not even your husband. I
>   know it looks like him but believe
>   me, there is nothing of the man you
>   loved in that car now. Nothing.

BEHIND we see ZOMBIE PHILIP reach forward and SWITCH THE
HARD HOUSE OFF. He sits back and looks almost peaceful.

We go from tragic drama to ironic comedy literally with the turn of a radio dial, yet both moments are properly grounded in character and circumstance. This abrupt but smooth shift in tone can be difficult to pull off in cross-genre projects like this. The first *Pirates of the Caribbean* film mastered this process beautifully, switching back and forth from comedy and drama to fantasy and horror, all the while still maintaining a believable world and characters. However, this franchise's sequels, which have gotten increasingly extreme, lurid and overdone, have lost their sense of realism; the characters and situations usually servicing their plots rather than the other way around.

Genre expectations and bending them

Crime comedy cross-genre films date back to as long ago as 1933's *The Little Giant* written by Robert Lord and Wilson Mizner, about a gangster bootlegger who sees his career ending with the repeal of prohibition and decides to get into high society. The film was a big hit starring gangster character actor Edward G Robinson, who would go on to make several more comedy gangster cross-genre films. These included the 1938 *A Slight Case of Murder* written by Earl Baldwin and Joseph Schrank, based on the play by Damon Runyon and Howard Lindsay; the 1940 *Brother Orchid* written by Earl Baldwin and Richard Connell; and the 1942 *Larceny Inc.* written by Everett Freeman and Edwin Gilbert and based on the play by Laura Perelman and S. J. Perelman. The crossing of these particular genres continued to thrive in the 1960s with the holiday classic gangster comedy *Pocket Full of Miracles* (1961) written by Hal Kanter and Harry Tuggend, based on a story by Damon Runyon; and the comedy crime musical *Robin and the 7 Hoods* (1964) written by David Schwartz and starring the Hollywood brat pack – Frank Sinatra, Dean Martin and Sammy Davis Jr. Crime and comedy have always been disciplines that can be merged well, but in most of these the crime element is only there for the sake of the comedy – there is no real heightened danger or traumatic death. If the audience comes in for a comedy, they usually won't want to watch people dying violently. In all of these crime comedies the criminal element is there, trying to commit a crime, but the comedy genre wins out.

Another crossing of the crime and comedy genres is the 2000 box office hit *Miss Congeniality* written by Marc Lawrence, Katie Ford, and Caryn Lucas. A serial killer has threatened a beauty pageant, so the FBI needs to send in an undercover agent as a contestant. Their choice for this important assignment is a total tom-boy who has no respect for the girlie girls who do beauty contests. While this is a thriller, the plot is laced with comedy as agent Grace Hart must learn how to become a beauty contestant or a girlie girl, and she is taught by a gay man of culture and style – everything she is not. Once again the cross in genres – thriller and comedy – is achieved through the characters. The thriller part of the story is never diminished or side-lined, but neither is the comedy which comes from our main character venturing into a world she is unfamiliar with and even hostile to – girls doing girlie things. While the potential for violence and death is hinted at all along, it is also side-lined for the sake of the comedy and the theme – finding yourself and embracing your femininity – something the female FBI agent must learn from her gay mentor.

This same mix of thriller and comedy was achieved years before in the 1991 hit film *The Hard Way* written by Lem Dobbs and Daniel Pyne. Here a serial killer is shooting up nightclubs in New York City and tough loner detective John Moss (James Woods) is after him. He's a man who can't keep a partner nor a girlfriend, but is suddenly forced to allow a young Hollywood movie star, Nick Lang, actor (Michael J Fox), tag along as research for his upcoming starring role as a NYC cop. Unlike the films of the past that mixed low crime and high comedy, this project includes people getting bloodily shot to heighten the danger and suspense. But neither of these films went as dark with its crime element as the famous screenplay written by Shane Black in 1987, *Lethal Weapon*. Parts of his script were considered too dark for audiences to stomach as a thriller action comedy and screenwriter Jeffery Boam rewrote it, adding more humor. In both of these films the violence is made tolerable for the audience thanks to the likability of the characters. These are people we enjoy spending two hours with, and these films bend the genre but still deliver the genre expectations.

To look at a harsher version of reinventing the basic design of a genre, we will examine the work of the masters of the form, Joel and Ethan Coen. All of their projects bend genre, usually with an element of dark comedy, from the farce and thriller aspects of *Fargo*, to the Cold War commentary and Hollywood shenanigans of *Hail Caesar!*, to the Preston Sturgess style hijinks and Odysseus structure of *O, Brother, Where art Thou*, to the western adventure and cross-country chase of *True Grit*. The results can be uneven or confusing, as in the spy thriller/woman in midlife crisis plot of *Burn After Reading*. However, when the elements the Coen's employ happen to mesh, they can mint story gold out of plot elements constructed of tin.

For example, the kidnapping, murders, and bizarre character machinations of 1996's *Fargo* shouldn't click together at all, but they do. As in the case of the best Coen movies and all the projects discussed in this chapter, if not this entire book, this is because the story ultimately focuses on a strong, accessible, and appealing protagonist. In *Fargo*, this is Marge, a pregnant Brainerd, Minnesota police chief investigating a murder case with multiple victims. We don't meet her until page 35 in the film's 105 page script, but she makes an indelible impression as she investigates a crime scene on a snow and corpse-littered country road with her colleague, Lou.

                    MARGE
          I'd be very surprised if our suspect was from Brainerd.

                    LOU
          Yah.

Marge is studying the ground intently.

                    MARGE
          Yah. And I'll tell you what, from his footprint
          he looks like a big fella –

Marge suddenly doubles over putting her head between her knees down near the snow.

                    LOU
          Ya see something down there, Chief?

                    MARGE
          Uh – I just, I think I'm gonna barf...

                    LOU
          Geez, you okay Margie?

                    MARGE
          I'm fine – it's just morning sickness –

She gets up, sweeping snow from her knees.

          ...Well, that passed.

We go from two police officers in a traditional scene based in familiar detective procedure to shocking farce in a single line and an indelible image: a uniformed, pregnant woman bent double over the snow. Again, this abrupt shift in tone and this weird mix of genres only works because the story is grounded in a believable and accessible character.

So why doesn't the script and the story start with Marge? Because of the film's genre – this is a police procedural. It's not a mystery and it's not really a thriller. The standard in caper films is to follow those pulling off the caper first and then introduce the cops trying to catch them. And the Coens adhere to those conventions here. But here's the bend to it. The person pulling of the crime is inept and a coward. His caper was to have his wife kidnapped and then make his rich father-in-law pay off and then split the money with the two goons he hired – all because he was going to be caught on a small fraud he was trying to unsuccessfully pull off at work. But everything goes wrong – the goons kill a cop and some innocent passers-by, the father-in-law refuses to pay, the goons turn on each other, and both his father-in-law and wife end up murdered. And when it's the right time within the genre's format to introduce the antagonist to the main character – the cop in a caper film – it's Marge. Not a threatening, seasoned detective, not a super sleuth, not a Dirty Harriet – but pregnant, slow talking, gentle Marge.

Fargo conforms to its genre, but what makes it so unique and so famous was how the Coen Brothers bent their project's crime genre, never truly crossing into comedy, but twisting it into a sardonic darkness.

A final note

Bottom line, the basic and most commercial genres of film and television, whether they're comic book, mystery, thriller, or science fiction, are alive and well but being realigned and recombined in surprising or unexpected permutations. Learn as much as you can about the particular genres that hold your interest – what their key elements are and how they work together – then tear them apart, reassemble them and make something new.

Mention must be made of how important it is for a screenwriter to be fully lettered or "viewed" in their respective area, no matter their preferred genre, discipline, or format. If you haven't seen any of the films or television series discussed in this book, then watch them and/or read their scripts as soon as you can. Educate yourself on their development and production histories from a variety of sources. At the least, read the Wikipedia pages that offer their basic information. Get a sense of the context of these projects; how similar films that followed or preceded them impacted their structure, story elements, and intentions. A broad knowledge of the antecedents that pertain to the screenplay or teleplay you're writing will be vital, especially when it's a cross-genre project. Creative context and circumstance is everything in this field, whether you are simply attempting to get the best possible return on this volume, writing your latest project, or working with experienced professionals on your first assignment.

To be blunt, when you've been hired to write a film noir slash horror project and your producer brings up *Chinatown* and *Psycho*, you don't want to respond with only a raised eyebrow and an anxious grin. Know your genres.

What did we learn?

Know your genre.
Love your genre.
Cross your genres.
Every story has a genre.

Exercise

Choose ten genres you are familiar with and lay them out in a table like the one below. Focus only on film or television genres you watch regularly and enjoy or you would be comfortable working with. If ten choices are too many then cut your list down to four, six or eight; whatever works for you, so long as it's an even number. For example:

- Drama
- Horror
- Science Fiction
- Western
- Thriller
- Comedy
- Family
- Political
- Historical
- War

Now examine premises you have previously written that focus on least five of these genres or create fresh ones; new or old, it doesn't matter. One way or another, you'll need five premises that match five of these genres for this exercise.

For simplicity's sake, let's say you have premises for the first five on this list – Drama, Horror, Science Fiction, Western, and Thriller. Now look at the remaining bottom five genres and rework each of your premises to match up with one of them. Like this . . .

- Drama/Family
- Horror/Comedy
- Science Fiction/War
- Western/Political
- Thriller/Historical

Even the immediate, undeveloped concepts we see here appear promising. Now focus on one of your mash-up premises, the one that appeals to you the most, and put further work into it. Develop it into a synopsis of a page or two. If any additional mash-ups work for you, develop them into synopses as well. If just one of these ideas shows any promise, then this has been an extremely successful exercise.

2 The write approach

Once we have a story, we need to decide on the style in which we are going to tell it. Will this be naturalistic, impressionistic, or surrealistic? Sometimes before we can write, and often after we've written a first draft, the angle on the story comes to us. How am I going to spin this tale? What will be the point of view? What approach will help tell the story the best? As an example, Jeff Nathanson was brought in to rewrite the screenplay for *The Terminal* (2004) because the producers and Steven Spielberg felt something was lacking – namely the basic approach to the plot. What they gave Nathanson was a story that all took place in the wing of an airport. Nathanson evaluated the story and considered it good but somehow stagnant thanks to the confines of the location, required by the plot. Then the approach came to him. It was like a prison movie. Here was the main character, trapped in a small place, unable to leave or to do much about it. Nathanson read the screenplays for *Shawshank Redemption* and other prison films and then went to work revising the screenplay with this approach in mind. What was there in prison stories that made them work and which could work for this story? Defeating the system, an unfeeling "warden," defiance? Nathanson now had an angle and he went to work. The producers, Stephen Spielberg and Tom Hanks loved it, and so did many film critics.

The co-writer of the inimitable *Citizen Kane* (1941), Herman J. Mankiewicz, spent many hours talking with the 19th-century newspaper tycoon William Randolph Hearst. He had done his research, and he knew he had a great story in this figure. He also had Orson Wells breathing down his neck to write the screenplay. But how to approach it? What should be the angle? He was stuck – until he settled on the idea of a mystery. What if the approach wasn't straightforward? What if he started the story with the main character's death and the whisper of a word – a word that no one knew what it meant or signified? Then he could explore this character's life from the point of view of reporters searching for the answer to the meaning of "Rosebud" and, along the way, tell the story of one man's life.

These are two examples of how writers came up with an approach, an angle from which to tell their stories. Finding your own angle on telling your own story will not only provide you with an approach, but often a stylistic manner in which to tell it.

Motivated style

Let us now examine Bill Condon's script for *Chicago* (2002). It's fair to say that Condon has redefined the American movie musical with this screenplay, just as Kander & Edd redefined the Broadway musical when it premiered under the choreography and direction of Bob Fosse. But Condon did more than just transcribe the play to the screen; he re-invented it with a motivated style.

Musical numbers should either further the plot or the characters' inner thoughts. In classics like Adolph Green and Betty Comden's *Singing in the Rain* and even in modern movie musicals like Dennis Potter's *Pennies from Heaven*, the musical numbers interrupt the dramatic scenes – or, in the case of *Evita*, are the dramatic scenes. But the musical numbers have always been given full and center stage when they occur. Not so with Condon. What he does is cross between the musical numbers and non-musical dramatic scenes, beginning at the start of the film as Velma sings in the night club and Roxie takes her lover to bed in her apartment. Condon writes in his screenplay every cut between these two moments as they simultaneously happen.

But that is not what is so original and impressive about Condon's writing. After all, cross-cutting between simultaneous actions is not uncommon, as in *The Godfather* murder/christening scene (which was actually created in the editing room long after the film was finished). Condon's true genius comes on page 16, when Roxie's husband Amos is confessing to the police that he killed a "burglar" – when in fact it was Roxie who killed him, and he was her lover.

```
Roxie sings the torch song leaning against the piano, a la
Helen Morgan. It's as if the only way for her to deal with
this terrifying situation is to transport herself to the
world she's always dreamed about - to see her life as
a vaudeville act.
```

From here on in, virtually every musical number will be just that – Roxie's inner emotional way to deal with the world crashing down around her. As Condon sets up his cross-cutting style with the first musical number, he's also established his logic and point of view for the rest of the film. Each and every musical number is an escape for Roxie (except one, which is an escape for Amos. But even this musical segment begins with Roxie staring out the back of an ambulance, "Roxie gazes out at Amos, a look of pity in her eyes").

So, from page 16 on, the cross-cutting isn't between simultaneous actions any more, it's between reality and Roxie's musical fantasy of a nightclub show. Her first night on death row she imagines herself in a club, "She takes a seat at a center table, an audience of one." The Cell Block Tango number is a highly stylized, Fosse-esque piece intercut with scenes of Roxie overhearing the real-life conversations of the various women of death row. The scene is a masterpiece, an excellent mix of great musical writing by Kander & Ebb, choreography, photography, art direction, editing and great performances.

But the thing that ties them all together is Condon's marvelous screenwriting, elevating the scene, and the movie, from a normal musical to an art film.

As Roxie internalizes her experiences, each moment is dramatized as a musical number, creating the motivation for the entire film. We witness this when she first sees lawyer Billy Flynn, when she's forced to answer questions before the press, when she talks with the prison Matron Mama about building a career in vaudeville, when Velma asks Roxie to be part of her act, when Billy takes her to her first day in court, and so on. Condon even adds musical interludes to scenes he created for the film – such as the surreal execution of the only innocent woman on death row, and Billy Flynn tap dancing his way out of trouble in court.

Without Condon's motivational concept that Roxie views everything as a vaudeville musical number as her coping device *Chicago* would just be a string of musical cabaret numbers on film – like *A Chorus Line*, which did not work well as a film. Stage musicals are all-encompassing – the dancing, the live music, the energy of a live performance. Much of that can become lost on the screen, again as in *A Chorus Line*.

Condon redefined what *Chicago* was about in its film version. Instead of it being a series of musical dance numbers strung together by a murderess's story, he created the very reason that this tale should be told as a musical in the first place. He gave a motivation for the musical numbers beyond the normal; they further the plot or the character's emotion. And, by doing so, he also gave a motivation for the style of the film – a snappy, jazzy, cross-cutting approach that fits the time period, the plot and, most of all, the main character. Condon made sure that everything in *Chicago*, including the style of the story telling, was motivated. Isn't that what every writer needs to do in any screenplay – musical or not?

The internal approach

Let us look at a non-musical approach. Akiva Goldsman worked hard on his screenplay for *A Beautiful Mind* (2001) to make us feel like his main character John did – through telling the story from John's point of view. This approach made the story all the more compelling and beautiful.

Making the audience experience the actual, tortured workings of the mind of a schizophrenic is a difficult task. Many films have been made about mentally ill protagonists. Most – such as *Equus, Shadow of a Doubt,* and *Pressure Point* – have been visualized from the point of view of an observer, a facilitator or medical professional; from someone on the outside looking in. Goldsman's challenge and his skill were getting us to "fall" for the same delusions that John himself believed are real. The audience knows going in that this is a story about a mentally ill genius. Goldsman thus uses abstract images to illustrate John's mind, revealing its twisted and delusional patterns. As he establishes John's anti-social and eccentric nature, we are lulled into believing that these are the ways that the screenwriter will illustrate John's craziness.

Thus we never suspect that his charming and helpful roommate is one of John's first and most long-standing hallucinations.

As the story progresses, John is recognized by others and by the audience as being a true genius and is asked to work on occasion with the Pentagon. Thus, when he is recruited to work on a top-secret project, who are we to doubt it? Slowly these realities become suspect. Then we begin to realize, only gradually, that they aren't real at all. We begin to experience the same doubts and sense of betrayal for being deceived as our main character does. We are inside his mind, sharing his insanity, not outside looking in.

Goldsman slowly sets everything up, piece by piece. Never do we see his roommate interact with anyone but John. Never does anyone see the little girl or the special agent. The lines between reality and his mind become blurred. But we never lose our focus on John's genius and his hidden depths. This is what attracts his wife Alicia to him and must be maintained in order for us to believe in their relationship. This is also a story of Alicia's incredible strength, not just standing with, but also fighting for her husband during his bouts with mental illness.

Goldsman slips in beautiful touches, such as the pen ceremony to honor great teachers which bookends the film, and John's relationship with his fellow classmates. To establish John's growth as a human being despite his mental afflictions, Sol, his colleague, and Hansen, his antagonist, both transform into his only friends by the story's third act.

Another example of how Goldsman keeps us in John's head is how he never allows John to be well. John merely learns to cope with his condition while he continues to have his imaginary friends follow him in various scenes. We feel John's triumph but also feel for his continuing battle with mental illness. *A Beautiful Mind* isn't only the biography of John Nash – it's a beautiful story thanks to the rich and imaginative point of view of the screenwriter who tells it.

Maintaining an established style

In all of these previous examples, the writers had the freedom to choose their basic approach to their material, even as they adapted their works from prior material. Needless to say, writers have complete freedom in their original projects to develop them in any style they see fit. Once directors, producers, cast and other collaborators become involved, the situation may change and the writer may be required to reinvent his approach to the project. But, at least at the beginning, the writer has some freedom in what he wants to do.

However, for the vast majority of writers who work in television, this is not the case. The show runner and/or creator of a series will establish the creative approach of the project and the writer(s) must mimic that style as best they can. This goes for the series' premise, world, story choice and characters, as well as the specific voices of those characters.

David Carren's (DC) first job in the industry was freelancing an episode of the original television version of *Starsky & Hutch* (1975–1979). When he brought in his first draft and his version of the lead characters did not sound or act like the lead characters that had been established in three seasons of the show, the story editor told him, "This show is called Starsky & Hutch, not 'A freelancer's characters'." This point, made in the 1970s, is still pertinent today. Every TV series has its own design in telling its specific story and it's the writer's job to copy that style as best he can while also still providing fresh energy and meat for the particular script he's working on; a difficult balancing act that is beyond the abilities of many wordsmiths. Each series must maintain its own creative method; this will be a key selling point to an audience deluged with choices. If the series doesn't stand out in its own unique way, why should anyone bother to watch it?

A strong example is available in the pilot for *The Walking Dead* (2010), written by Frank Darabont, based on the graphic novel by Robert Kirkman. In one of the first scenes in the series set at night, the point-of-view hero, Rick Grimes, witnesses a walker approach his hiding place in a house.

```
RICK'S POV

A WALKER is drifting up the lawn toward us. A woman. Her skin,
once black, now the color of dead fish.

RICK

Pulls back. It's like she knows they're inside. In fact, as he
watches, she changes course from the window and drifts toward
the front door.

Rick loses sight of her. He leaves the slit, eases to the door
instead. Listens. Barely breathing.

He puts his eye to the peephole.

PEEPHOLE POV (FISHEYE LENS)

The woman is just outside, wildly distorted in the fisheye
effect. Turning her head, also listening.

She reaches her hand out toward the door, and:

Soft scratching. She wants in.
```

The style is immediate and striking. Capped character names or POV indicate shots. Brief and telling lines of description express visual beats. Key moments are underlined. The writing is lean but dramatic and intensive, an approach that will define every episode of the entire series of *The Walking Dead*. While elements, characters, and situations may change, any writer that creates a script for this show will be required to follow in Daramont's footsteps from now on, at least when it comes to its basic narrative style.

It's a TV writer's job to become a craftsman whose work will be distinct to a particular show, a chameleon whose colors must change to suit the job at hand. If they can't perform that function, they won't last long working for that series or any other. The challenge in creative assimilation in television will always be the same.

Style that fits the genre

It is interesting that part of the approach here is how Daramont also made the style of his writing match the genre he was writing. Zombies are slow, creepy and, because of these attributes, most zombie stories have slow-building suspense. Part of the fun of the zombie movie is the slow build to the bloody climax – the creeping doom. The way Daramont lays out the action in short sentences, how he adds spaces between them, creates for the reader a similar feeling of growing doom that the end resulting TV show will have. The writing approach fits the genre.

Russo and Elliot did the same when penning *Pirates of the Caribbean*, writing in the same flippant and fun style that they envisioned the movie to have. John August did it in *Big Fish*, writing as if his script was in itself a tall tale. The fashion in which we write and the words we writers choose is as important as the story we tell and the characters we create. The style of the writing will help create in the minds of all who read it – producers, directors, actors, art directors, costume designers, cinematographers, editors, and composers – the tone of the movie they see in their minds when they read the script. And with any luck, they will carry that tone into the finished production.

What did we learn?

Find the right style.
Motivate it.
Maintain it
Research it.
Support it with a strong and appropriate theme.
Fit your style to your genre.

Exercise

Write a scene in your own style, or at least one that you're comfortable with. Place two characters in a dramatic moment in a location with which you are familiar. You can set the scene in your own workplace or a family situation, using the voices, attitudes, and situation of people you know.

Now take that same scene and set it in a supposed episode of a television show of your choosing. Track down a script for the series you wish to emulate and make sure the format and style of your scene matches the show's approach. Adjust your own characters, their drama, their history and their voices to match certain key characters in the series. Depending on the scene you've written and the series you've chosen, you should find the revision process pretty challenging.

Another way to approach this is to simply write a scene blind for a TV series you appreciate or enjoy, then read a production draft from the show and see how you managed or didn't manage to copy the show's style. If you didn't do well, write a new scene to better match that style. This will give you a preview into working in television. Whatever the circumstance, whichever the show, you will be expected to read previous production drafts and match or imitate their approach in your own work. This can also occur on film assignments as well, especially if you're scripting a sequel, prequel or reboot of a prior property. Depending on the project, as a creative chameleon, your colors will have to change.

3 Character depth

It's a given that no story, whatever its format, market, setting, or medium, can work if its characters fail to engage, surprise, or appeal to the project's audience. But remember that "engage" only happens when the story and its theme properly support the characters, "surprise" only works when the discovery is earned, and "appeal" doesn't mean "like" so much as identify with.

Motivating your characters

Part of why *Pirates of the Caribbean: The Curse of the Black Pearl* (2003), written primarily by Ted Elliott & Terry Rossio, works so well is in the manner in which its key characters are so carefully employed in service to its theme through the creation of people who are successfully engaging, surprising and appealing to the audience. In this case, the well-structured plot and carefully nurtured themes provide the sharply defined characters with the obstacles and challenges they need to grow, change, and progress.

Great screen storytelling doesn't give its people easy solutions to their problems, and *Pirates*' lovers, Elizabeth Swann and Will Turner, find themselves faced with seemingly insurmountable obstacles. It's established in the very first scene when a pre-teen Elizabeth wishes to meet a pirate and then her desire comes true. However, she is forced to spend the rest of the film securing him against the strictures of her class, the opposition of the pirates, and her lover's own instincts. Will, who is deeply ashamed of his lowly position in Port Royale's social strata, does not feel he deserves Elizabeth, let alone be able to even call her by her first name, and, as he learns his father was a pirate, he's even more convinced of this reality.

Mention must also be made of the significance of a pirate movie having its key point of view character and protagonist, from the very first scene, a young woman. This is not only highly unusual for a pirate project, it's not the usual approach for any action adventure film. The fact that the entire story is focused on Elizabeth achieving the freedom to be who she wants and love who she wants is not only appropriate for a female character living in the mid-17th century, it's unfortunately still relevant to today.

Beyond Elizabeth and Will, even the darkest characters in *Pirates* understand the value of individual freedom. The key villain, Barbossa, has a strong motivation that relates to the film's central theme of achieving personal freedom; he simply wants to be human again, as defined by his desire to eat a green apple (green signifying life as opposed to red, signifying blood or death). Jack Sparrow, as he so eloquently expresses to Elizabeth when they're marooned on an island together, says the Black Pearl represents freedom to him, which is clearly what he's seeking throughout the film.

Jack's character is a particularly surprising and almost unique creation. He's a trickster, not unlike Puck in *A Midsummer Night's Dream*, and he's wily, shocking, and unpredictable; all very appealing and scarce qualities in an action adventure movie character. His single-minded determination to retrieve his ship drives him through the story and pulls other characters, particularly Will, along with him. Yet though he's a pirate and ostensibly a bloodthirsty renegade, he never actually hurts an innocent person anywhere in the story. Please regard the list of Jack's "crimes" the magistrate reads off when he's about to be hung – not one of them is a violent act against another human being. As Elizabeth herself says, Jack managed to sack the port of Panama without firing a single shot. The man is not a killer, he's a rascal; an important distinction that allows the audience to adore him.

Barbossa, on the other hand, is a more typical pirate. Like Jack, he's a trickster, sly of tongue and action, broad and appealing in his own way, but far more ruthless. For while it's clear Jack can't be trusted – he lies as easily as he breathes – the man never betrays anyone at the level Barbossa, his former first mate, betrayed him. What's worse, Barbossa is a demon of the night, describing himself with great eloquence as a walking ghoul, and he even has a demon's familiar, the monkey, as a constant reminder of his damnation. However, his hunger for just one satisfying bite of that green apple humanizes him.

Screenwriters take note; black and white characterization is a disastrous choice in film – just look at the three *Star Wars* prequels George Lucas launched onto the world. In those movies, all of the people are either totally good or utterly evil with no shades in between, leaving the audience with nothing but plot mechanics and special effects to hang on to. *Pirates of the Caribbean* brilliantly avoided this trap.

A final few character notes. Take a close look at Mullroy and Murtogg, the two British Marines that Jack first encounters on the *Interceptor*'s dock. In reality, the 18th century's British Marines were fearless soldiers, the best of the best, just like today's United States Marines. When we meet these guys they're shading themselves under the dock, arguing like schoolboys and are as easily gulled. These are not genuine British Marines; they're a couple of overgrown kids.

On the other side of the equation, the two pirates Pintell and Ragetti are no more mature or realistic. Even though they're vicious killers, they're still childlike and playful, bickering like two bullies in a playground, and they're as easily misled as the silly Marines. Murtogg and Mullroy and Pintell and Ragetti are "twins" to each other – matching sets of juvenile characters that provide comedy relief and structural support throughout the film. Compare them to the boring supporting players in so many action films and you can see how they provide a welcome energy to exposition and narrative in a dozen places.

Finally, please examine Norrington and the elder Swann, Elizabeth's father. These characters are failed people in the sense they cannot change. Elizabeth and Will face their destiny with courage and adaptability, bravely overcoming every obstacle and reverse thrown their way by pirates, society and circumstance. By the end of the film, Elizabeth is commanding a ship in major combat at sea while Will has finally accepted his life mate. Norrington and Swann, on the other hand, have experienced almost nothing in a true emotional sense and changed nothing. The only false note in the entire plot is when Norrington releases all of our heroes at the end of the story, a choice no doubt dictated by audience expectation.

Also, keep close track of the gold medallion that Elizabeth takes from Will, which she then retrieves from her bedroom drawer (leaving a dust trail, showing it's been there a long time) and then drops in the ocean with her. All good stories offer a sense of destiny, and the medallion is the McGuffin for the heroine's destiny. It binds Elizabeth to Will, and then brings the pirates to Port Royale at a key point in the plot. It defines the pirates' goal as well as Elizabeth's. And it's neat and visual.

Films, especially genre films, are rife with elements like this. From small items like the Maltese Falcon to world-sized things like the *Titanic*; the stronger such an element can be, the stronger your story, characters and theme.

Switching to subtext – the emotion and ideas beneath a scene as opposed to the text; the basic information being dealt with or conveyed – *Pirates* offers us a solid education in this area as well. If a writer wants to see how subtext can be used brilliantly in a character scene to not only service that particular beat but the central theme of an entire film, take a hard look at the moment early in the script between Elizabeth and her maid Estrella in her bedroom.

It begins with the maid showing her concern: "It was a difficult day for you I'm sure." Now remember – Elizabeth fell off a cliff and almost drowned before a filthy pirate wrapped a chain around her throat and pointed a pistol at her head. Any rational person would assume Estrella is referring to any or part of these horrific events. But Elizabeth thinks her maid is commenting on Norrington's marriage proposal. "I must admit I wasn't entirely prepared for it." Estrella then corrects Elizabeth, saying she was actually talking about "being threatened by that pirate" and only then does Elizabeth say "Oh. Yes. It was terrifying."

It's clear. For Elizabeth, being married to Norrington is literally a fate worse than death. She'd rather Jack had killed her.

The scene continues with Estrella offering, "if it's not too bold" that the Commodore is a good match. When Elizabeth half-heartedly agrees, saying Norrington is the kind of man any woman "should" marry, Estrella takes note, offering that Will Turner's a fine man, too. Elizabeth gives her maid a sharp look and snaps, "That is too bold." She's putting Estrella in her place. But Estrella just smiles and slips the knife in by saying, "Begging your pardon, miss. It was not my place." What she's really saying to Elizabeth is that it's not *her* place to love Will Turner.

In less than a page of superb work, we touch on the central conflict of the entire script – freedom versus imprisonment – and our point of view character's central dilemma – how can she ever have her pirate? This also clearly helps establish that Elizabeth is our protagonist – it is her story, goals, change, and journey into the unknown. She is the one that makes the entire story happen.

Screenwriters take note. Never state the obvious. Slip in behind your characters and let them express their greatest desires and fears through subtext. And remember – creating characters that engage, surprise, and appeal to an audience is not as simple as it sounds.

Unmasking your characters

Have you ever heard the saying that the characters in your screenplay should be like an onion? No, we're not saying they should bring tears to your eyes or give you bad breath. We mean they should be multilayered and, during the course of your story, the outer layers should be peeled off to reveal what's inside. This is, of course, easier said than done. Writers need to learn or establish a lot about their characters in order to find what's inside. Most of us don't even know enough about ourselves to discover our own true natures, which may be why writing layered characters can be therapeutic. But we'll leave that to the trained professionals who charge by the hour.

There is something known in writing circles as the character mask. This is when a character presents one appearance, but eventually another truer self is revealed later on. Let's take a deeper look at the modern classic film which launched George Lucas's career, along with the careers of quite a number of now-famous actors; *American Graffiti* (1973), one of the best ensemble movies ever made.

In this film, screenwriters George Lucas, Gloria Katz and Willard Huyck wrote an engaging story of a group of high school graduates as they experience their last day of summer. What makes their screenplay stand out is their clever use of character masks to tell a fresh, surprising and fun story of the coming of age. The movie tracks basically four plot lines: the couple who have it all together, the wise guy in doubt, the nerd with a pretense of self-assurance, and the cool guy with the air of indifference. All four main characters are friends, their comfortable relationships in flux with the departure of two of them being college-bound, but all of them living behind masks, concealing who they really are from not only each other but from themselves as well. The events of the evening during which the story unfolds change them by forcing them to re-examine who they really are. As the screenplay flows back and forth between each character's experiences, we see layer after layer fall away until they all begin to change their outlook on life and themselves.

This is all achieved through a series of simple scenes that illustrate the experiences of a typical high schooler's night on the circuit, cruising the town's main drag. Throughout this action, the film's writers skillfully embed humor in the character's experiences – as when the nerd obtains a cool car to drive around in and a pretty or "easy" blonde girl suddenly hops into the seat beside him. But when they go necking, the car is stolen and the nerd must come to grips with his true self – as a loser and not part of the cool gang. The easy girl becomes the mirror before which he can drop his mask, for, instead of the stereotype dumb blonde, the screenwriters make her a three-dimensional person who has her own ideas, concerns and insights. It is under her encouragement that the nerd finally attempts to make a stand and take back the stolen car. And as he begins to fail, as only he could, it is the "dumb" blonde that comes to his aid. Together they succeed and realize that neither is as simple a character as they may have perceived themselves to be. Their changes are subtle, not a total makeover, but it gives both of them new energy and encouragement to face the world.

In the same manner, the writers use a mask with their hot rod cool guy. While trying to impress the ladies driving on the drag, he ends up with a young tweenie in his car. Embarrassed to even be seen with her, he attempts to dump the girl, but then his mask of cool indifference begins to slip and their relationship grows to one of enjoying each other's company. Instead of the hot womanizer persona he prefers to display, Mr. Hot Rod allows himself to become the gentle big brother he is deep inside. It is this awaking that leads him to the realization that he shouldn't waste his life on drag racing.

The writers also give their wise guy character an impossible quest – the search for that gorgeous woman who whispered "I love you" while driving past him on the drag in a white convertible T-bird. She's an unachievable fantasy he can use to stop himself from moving on, from leaving town and facing the future and college, which he obviously fears. By his pursuing this unobtainable goal, the writers allow the wise guy to face a more dangerous obstacle – the street gang. Using his wit, he is able to turn the tables on them, transforming himself from captive to honorary member. As he proves his personal bravery to them, and eventually himself, he realizes he can face the future and head off to college for whatever lies ahead.

The perfect couple are the past school president and homecoming queen. They appear to have their future together all planned out, but the writers make their nice, smart, always-in-control guy do something that will force the situation beyond his control. He logically explains to his steady that they should feel free to see someone else while college separates them. He explains this to her and to himself as simple logic. She reflects his cold logic back at him and makes him question his decision and motives. The mirror she holds up to his mask forces him to lower it and take the risk of looking inside and realizing that, for once, he is unsure.

In this one night, these four main characters are given the opportunity to remove their masks to breathe some fresh, clean air. Isn't this what we all long to do as human beings? Perhaps this is why this film resonated so deeply with the public when it was first released and even through to the current day. The writers of *American Graffiti* used the character mask as the backbone of their story to create a full-bodied screenplay. They let each onion peel back a few layers and, if it forced the audience to shed any tears, they were of enjoyment. So don't be afraid to peel a layer or two off your own personal onion; if it produces a few tears, so much the better.

Humor is character

Life is not devoid of humor. Why should screenplay dramas be any different? *Catch Me if You Can* (2002) is not a comedy. Jeff Nathanson's screenplay, which is based on the autobiography of con-artist and check forger Frank Abagnale, is really a story of a boy who longs to find a place where he belongs and a relationship where he can be himself. This is a true crime story that begins with a dysfunctional family consisting of a son, his father and a less than affectionate mother. While this could easily be a psychological crime drama, Nathanson's skill of expanding on the truth also allowed him to add touches of humor that made the story all the more human.

The plot begins with a gloomy tone in a dim world – the horrible conditions of a French prison and the near-death condition of Frank, the prisoner FBI agent who Carl is here to extradite. To offset this darkness, Nathanson preludes the screenplay with a segment of the old TV show *To Tell the Truth* in which Frank was the guest. This helps to establish the film's true tone and premise, that of a brilliant individual playing an entertaining if desperate game. After the prison scene, Nathanson transports us into the past to reveal the ugly collapse of Frank's home life. He gives us the first humorous insight into Frank's personality when his parents are called into the high school principal's office where they are told: "Mr. And Mrs. Abagnale, this is not a question of your son's attendance. I regret to inform you that for the past week, Frank has been teaching Ms. Glasser's French Class."

Even as the parent conference continues, Frank offers a fellow student tips on how to make her fake doctor's note appear more convincing. Frank's ingenuity is quickly established and sets the tone for the rest of the story; one that includes a father without values, a mother who has an affair and abandons her son, and a boy who is forced to live alone without the ability to earn a living. It should be no huge surprise that a desperate, smart kid like

Frank, raised by people with little character or true humanity, would resort to forging checks to feed and clothe himself.

Audiences love to root for the underdog, especially one who beats the system. This is the character Nathanson skillfully sets up in his writing, adding a troubled soul into the mix, making Frank more three-dimensional and engaging. This is no light subject for a movie. *Catch Me if You Can* is the story of a boy pretending to be a man in order to steal to survive – a boy who gets no guidance whatsoever from his parents, who are only concerned for themselves. Nathanson re-introduces Carl, the FBI agent, 20 minutes after we first saw him, as the antagonist who hunts down Frank. But Carl will also fill the void left by Frank's father, becoming the only man who truly cares about the boy.

In a way, Frank gives Carl something important as well – a purpose, a project, and a goal. These characters are set up as opposites: Frank the free-wheeling, anything goes, fun-loving young con-artist, and Carl, the mature, deadpan, ultra-serious workaholic. What they both share is a loneliness that Nathanson reveals beautifully by having Frank call up Carl at the FBI offices on Christmas Eve. To hammer home the significance of the situation, Nathanson even has Frank tell Carl exactly where he is staying. But Carl, alone in his office with a photo of his ex-wife and child, refuses to believe him. This is such a skillfully written scene it skips over being manipulative into true melancholy and pathos.

All that said, the story is never completely devoid of humor. Nathanson uses Carl, the least humorous character in the film, to provide the most laughs. When the other agents make fun of Carl, he tells them a knock-knock joke that ends with "Who's there? Go Fuck yourself!" The fact that the joke isn't funny is what actually makes it so funny. It's a startling, even shocking moment for this straight-laced character. The unexpected, whether it's action, story twists, characters or dialogue, is what we all strive for in our writing. The unexpected is what makes the world and life so interesting.

Nathanson's script is full of surprises – from the ingenuity of Frank's con games, to the relentlessness of Carl's pursuit, to the growth of their unexpected father/son relationship. There are very few laugh-out-loud moments in the film, yet the humor and fun of the story prevails, even within the tragic circumstances of its characters. It is with small dashes of humor that Nathanson makes the drama hit its mark so much more poignantly. We all want to be able to do that – to write it if we can.

The other character change

Aristotle, in his *Poetics*, basically said that good stories feature a main character who changes and if they don't they are doomed to suffer for it or perhaps even die. Everyone talks about the character arc and how their goals change as the story progresses. In order to reach their goal the character must change. But there can also be another version of character change. One such screenplay that does this quite well is the comedy *Miss Congeniality* (2000) written by Marc Lawrence, Katie Ford, and Caryn Lucas.

The story is about a tomboy FBI agent who gets assigned to pose as a beauty contestant in order to stop someone threatening to blow it up. It's a fish-out-of-water story, with the hard-as-nails Agent Gracie Harte being picked by her superior Agent Matthews to go undercover as Miss New Jersey (of course). But when her superior, Agent Eric Matthews, offers her the job, she is somewhat resistant at first to put it mildly.

>   ERIC MATTHEWS
> What do you say, Hart?
>
>   GRACIE HART
> No freakin' way.
>
>   ERIC MATTHEWS
> Sparky, why not?
>
>   GRACIE HART
> Cause I'm not gonna parade around in a swimsuit like
> some airhead bimbo that goes by the name, what,
> Gracie Lou Freebush, and all she wants is world peace?
>
>   ERIC MATTHEWS
> It won't be like that. Come on, you're an important
> member of the undercover team.
>
>   GRACIE HART
> Yeah, right, in a thong.

But a makeover isn't the only thing the writers settled for in their character change. They avoided the "ugly duckling to swan" as the character's main change and the "now she's hot and attracting all the men" angle and instead decided that her change was in how she viewed women who she thought to be vacant, looks obsessive, fools. Her change was to recognize that everyone is an individual and that every person has inherent worth and value. That's a big change, and one worthy of being made for any character. Does this change solve the case? No, it doesn't. The physical makeover is the change that allows her to blend in and catch the criminal. While the plot focuses on her mission and the humor of her being unfamiliar with how to look and act like a feminine woman and not let her hard edges show, it also gently allows her to discover what she's been missing most of her life – female companionship and comradery. So in this case, instead of her true character change allowing her to reach her goal, her inner character change was a byproduct of trying to reach her goal. Pursuing her goal allowed her to discover the woman inside herself and forced her to build relationships with the kind of people she avoided or discounted.

It is important that the writers never allowed Gracie to fully change and embrace what the other women embrace nor fully become one of them. They recognized doing that would be too trite, and unbelievable. At the end of the film, she doesn't dress more stylishly or frilly and doesn't wear fine-tuned make-up, but she does take a bit more care with her appearance. The internal change begins to show itself in the third act of the script in the well-set-up interview part of the pageant; the moment that her beauty pageant mentor Victor had been dreading the most, that puts Agent Gracie in the spotlight.

>KATHY MORNINGSIDE
>New Jersey, as you know, there are many who consider the Miss United States Pageant to be outdated and anti-feminist. What would you say to them?
>
>GRACIE HART
>Well, I would have to say – I used to be one of them. And then I came here and I realized that these women are smart, terrific people who are just trying to make a difference in the world. And we've become really good friends. I mean, I know we all secretly hope the other one will trip and fall on her face and – wait a minute, I've already done that! And for me this experience has been one of the most rewarding and liberating experiences of my life.

The Audience applauds as Victor watches.

>VICTOR MELLING
>My God, I did it!
>
>GRACIE HART
>And if anyone, anyone – tries to hurt one of my new friends I would take them out. I would make them suffer so much that they'd wish they were never born. And if they ran, I would hunt them down. Thank you, Kathy.
>
>VICTOR MELLING
>A brief shining moment, and then that mouth!

How much a character changes is as important as how the character changes. Gracie always remains true to herself – that being a hard-edged tomboy dedicated to law enforcement. It is her view of others that has changed, and that changes her behavior as well. Of course, she doesn't win the pageant which she was never trying to do, but she wins something much more important that shows her inner change. She wins the Miss Congeniality award from her fellow contestants, the very women she originally held distain for but has now come to see as people and friends.

It's not a reward for saving lives or solving the case, it's a reward for changing her perspective on life. Seeing a character make small steps forward, seeing them begin to change for the better, gives us all hope that we too can and will begin to change. And that's a character change worth writing about.

Television characters

With the current new Golden Age of television – over 450 series in production and counting – a discussion of character in this medium is even more topical if not required. A film's characters, at least outside of potential sequels, prequels, and remakes, are usually finite. If the falling action of the resolution has been properly achieved, the audience may experience a satisfying afterglow regarding the characters' fictional futures, but, when the story ends, their lives end, in a way. With television projects, the primary goal is to maintain an intriguing cast of characters throughout an extended period of dramatic time; one that could cover as many as ten seasons or more. Until recently, most TV series managed this within a contained, simple episodic format with each segment standing mostly if not entirely on its own. An issue would be introduced, dramatized, and resolved in an hour or half hour and that was that. You could watch an episode of *The Mentalist, The Simpsons,* or *Southpark,* and pretty much follow what was going on without any serious confusion or dissatisfaction over context, character, or plot.

Today, most TV series have a serial aspect to them, or at least an overall arc that displays or exploits new aspects of the characters from season to season. This approach demands a much deeper development of the show's people and a much more complex exploration of its story, worlds, and themes. This has led to a startling wave of experimentation and innovation in the dramatic development of television, as displayed in ambitious projects like *Lost, The Walking Dead, Breaking Bad,* and *Game of Thrones* that have arguably revolutionized the process. Not only are the characters more complex but their worlds as well, whether it's a zombie apocalyptic landscape, a remote, magical island, or an alternate universe Dark Ages.

Needless to say, this has generated an unprecedented level of artistic and professional pressure for today's television writers. While it's never been an easy matter creating multiple episodes of a TV series, whether it's keeping the characters' voices and behavior consistent, the production quality at a proper level, or simply getting each segment shot and edited in time for their air dates, you add in the new creative and budgetary demands of today's incredibly competitive market (450 series!) and the challenge can be truly overwhelming.

In this current envrionment, it's no longer adequate to offer "likable" characters in a normal contemporary world in a simple episodic format. A much more multifaceted, often darker approach is required. Look at *Mad Men*'s Don Draper, an utterly amoral individual who stole the identity of a dead war hero and never met a woman he wouldn't betray, *Breaking Bad*'s Walter White who went from mild-mannered chemistry teacher to ruthless meth baron in six seasons, or all of the people in *Game or Thrones*, every one of them capable of almost any crime or barbarity depending on their circumstance or situation. Brett Martin, in his book *Difficult Men: Behind the Scenes of a Creative Revolution: From The Sopranos and The Wire to Mad Men and Breaking Bad*, has focused on the male component of this phenomenon. But a quick look at series like *Scandal, Orange Is the New Black, Homeland*, and *Crazy Ex-Girlfriend* will reveal that the female sex is just as capable of multifarious difficulty and acrimony in today's television.

The British series *Peaky Blinders* (2013–) is an excellent example of this new paradigm. Set in Birmingham, England, right after World War I and focused on the activities of a real-life criminal gang named the Peaky Blinders (so called for the razor blades sewn into the peaks of their flat caps,) this series checks all the boxes discussed so far – an unusual world, difficult characters, and a demanding serial story structure. While the period is properly addressed to the point that a young Winston Churchill even makes an appearance, the plot focuses on a family of Peaky Blinders, the Shelbys, and its rising star, the ruthless Thomas Shelby, a veteran of the Great War who is determined to take his clan from the grit and grime of the Small Heath tenements to a brighter future no matter the means, whether it be gambling, gun running, grand larceny or murder.

Thomas is a taciturn, bitter man, his actions literally speaking louder than words. When he buys a bottle of rum from a young woman, Grace, who has just started working at his local pub (a character who will become his love interest in future episodes,) we do not have anything like the usual boy-meets-girl moment.

```
She finds a bottle of dark rum and puts it onto the bar.

                    GRACE
          Harry said on the house.

Thomas pushes the coins forward then peers at Grace.

                    THOMAS
          Are you a whore?

Grace is astonished. Thomas stares at her.

                    THOMAS (CONT'D)
          Because if you're not, you're in
          the wrong place.

Thomas takes the bottle of rum and leaves.
```

Thomas is fearlessly honest and brazen and not just with bar girls but with every aspect of his business and family. When he stumbles on a crate filled with mislaid government munitions that the police are tearing the city apart to find, he doesn't do the sensible thing and dump it. He decides to sell or barter it back to the British, a reckless gambit that would appall even his Aunt Polly, the equally ruthless matriarch of the Shelby clan. But he resists her demands to come clean on his plans in a family-meeting scene that works through several levels, as does every scene in every episode of the series.

```
Polly now has deep suspicions that Thomas knows more than he
is saying. She gets to her feet...

                    POLLY
        This family does everything open.
        You have nothing more to say to
        this meeting, Tommy?

Silence. Thomas feels her suspicion and meets her stare.

                    THOMAS
        Nothing that's women's business.

Polly stares back with cool certainty...

                    POLLY
        This whole bloody enterprise was
        "women's business"' while you boys
        were away at war. What's changed?

Thomas is equally cool as he gestures around...

                    THOMAS
        We came back.
```

In this one moment, we have historical context (how the Great War affected the characters), the family's dynamics (Thomas is its true power center,) and recognition of a key element of the plot (foreshadowing on the crate of guns). This is modern television in the new Golden Age personified in a few lines in just one scene in one episode of one series. Without complex characters, world, and story, no writer need apply.

What did we learn?

Bone up on the "rules" Aristotle laid out 2,500 years ago about protagonists, antagonists, plot points, conflict, character is action, and so forth.
Break the rules if you like but be sure you know them first.

Give your characters masks, then rip them off.

Characters in television today are more often than not carefully developed to sustain involved, daring, and dramatic story lines that could support several seasons.

Humor is character.

Exercise

If you are in the midst of a screenplay, write personal histories of at least two key characters – such as your antagonist, protagonist, love interest, mentor, key ally, etc. Get as detailed as you can – where they were born, their favorite food, their best friend, the worst and best moments in their life, etc. Each of these breakdowns should be as long as a detailed premise – at least two or three pages. Arrive at a key moment in their lives that made them who they are and explore it specifically in this breakdown, then script it as a scene, whether it belongs in your script or not. However you design your characters and story, the information you develop should be useful.

If you are not currently working on a script then write your own history as well as that of a parent, loved one or best friend. Be as honest as you can and focus on what you feel really matters, what made you and the other person who they are. Then take the most interesting moment you remember from each of these histories and turn them into premises for a story. You may be pleasantly surprised with what you come up with.

4 Dialogue that does more than further the plot

```
"What we've got here is failure to communicate."

"I'll make him an offer he can't refuse."

"Frankly, my dear, I don't give a damn."

"R-o-s-e-b-u-d."

"Badges? We ain't got no badges! We don't need no badges!
I don't have to show you any stinkin' badges!"

"Show me the money!"
```

When we think of a movie we recall it like a dream. We see faces and flashes, a sequence of action, a moment of dire peril or intense passion, a gorgeous countryside or an alien world. When it comes to the dialogue of a film, we'll remember a sentence, an exchange, and a fragment of talk – such as with the examples above – that may be particularly notable, striking or haunting. For the viewer, the context could get entirely lost, the character who spoke the line forgotten, its position in the story misplaced. For an inexperienced writer, the danger arises in the notion that great dialogue is great lines, just a few perfectly chosen and arranged words, or a brilliantly structured speech or sentence living all on its own – which couldn't be further from the truth.

Like every element in a well-written script, dialogue is not a stand-alone element that functions in isolation. It's part of a carefully crafted whole, a key piece in the elaborate puzzle of every intelligently developed TV episode and movie. Every word and speech must enhance, support, and progress the characters, plot and intention of the entire project. And the dialogue must accomplish this while also entertaining, enlightening, and/or surprising the audience. Managing a story and its characters while creating riveting scenes that still produce an accessible, natural, and inevitable result is a challenge many new writers can never successfully achieve.

One of the reasons for this could be that the finished, professional productions they view appear to be so seamless and inevitable in their construction and intention. It looks easy but it wasn't. Creating a well-spoken script with dialogue that smoothly supports and enhances its characters and story is no simple task.

A distinct voice

An examination of a key scene from the teaser of "Ozymandias" (2013), Moira Walley-Beckett's Emmy winning episode of *Breaking Bad* (2008–2013) – a script many critics have hailed as one of, if not the, greatest scripts ever written for a television series – might be helpful in illustrating the challenges of good dialogue successfully feeding character and plot.

"Ozymandias" is the 60th episode of *Breaking Bad*, the 14th of the fifth season, and a story that takes place near the climax of the entire series. Walter White's dangerous and ruthless career as a meth producer has reached its ugly resolution with a group of his associates murdering his brother-in-law, Hank, as well as Hank's partner, in a violent desert standoff. However, the episode begins in an extremely daring place: the moment when Walt, while cooking his first batch of meth in his old RV in the exact same patch of desert, makes a call to his wife, and tells his first lie. It's a seemingly simple and natural scene but it works on so many narrative levels. Within the context of the episode, it's a moment that speaks to the path Walt is about to follow and how it will affect him and his relationship with his wife at that particular moment. Within the context of the series, it's a comment on the entire, terrible journey that Walt has taken, illustrating the bitter fruit of his endeavors – a dead brother-in-law, a shattered marriage, and a barrel of money.

The scene is also filmic and colorful in a subtle way; contrasting the world of Walt's RV desert lab with his wife Skyler's neat, clean kitchen where she is packaging a family heirloom she sold on eBay for a pittance. This adds an extra level of irony to the scene: Walt is making meth to eventually earn literally millions of dollars while Skyler is trolling eBay for a few bucks.

The scene starts in a manner familiar to any husband and wife ...

> SKYLER
> Hello.
>
> WALT
> Hi, Honey, it's me.
>
> SKYLER
> Hi, you. What's going on?

Skyler is cheerful and light-hearted – easy-breezy. God, we haven't seen her this way in so long. Walt musters himself, then launches into his lie – his very first major lie to his wife:

> WALT
> Nothing much. I, uh ... I just called to say that I'm sorry, but I'm going to be late tonight. It's Bogdan, he's got a bug up his –

                    SKYLER
    (interrupts) That's okay, I don't have anything special
    planned for dinner. You won't be missing much.

Skyler's unconcerned – she has no reason not to trust him – Walt
being late is no big deal. Walt's relieved – exhales some of his
stress.

                    SKYLER
    In fact, I may ask you to take pity on us and bring home
    a pizza. They have a two-for-one at Venezia's. At this point,
    I could eat a whole one all by myself.

                    WALT
    Sure, I can grab pizza. Hopefully Bogdan won't keep me too
    late.

                    SKYLER
    He better not – trust me, he does not want to piss off
    a hungry pregnant woman.

She tapes the box – BRRRRRAAAAP.

                    WALT
    What's that sound?

                    SKYLER
    I just sold your favorite piece – the hideous crying
    clown. Got nine bucks more than I paid for it, too.

In their respective locations, both of them smile.

                    WALT
    Shows what I know about art.

                    SKYLER
    Oh – what do you think of Holly? (off his confused
    silence) For the baby's name. Do you like it? I think
    I really like it.

                    WALT
    Holly. It's nice. (considers) Lemme think about it.

                    SKYLER
    Just kinda feels right, you know? It's my new favorite.

                    WALT
    It's a frontrunner, for sure.

The scene goes on for a moment longer as Walt talks with Skyler about their having some family time that weekend, he agrees to name their unborn daughter Holly, they express their love for each other, and the moment is over. Then Walt, the RV, and Jesse fade away, leaving only empty desert.

In three pages, look at how much ground has been covered, how many issues are addressed to service the story, the characters, and the entire series. The text of the scene is fairly simple – Walt is telling his wife he will be coming home late while she boxes up an item for eBay and she asks him to bring home a pizza. The subtext is multi-layered; he's telling her his first lie that will lead to thousands more that will eventually result in the destruction of his entire world. To add poignancy, we learn when the two decided on their new baby's name. Even the mention of pizza has an extra added frisson – in another episode a furious Walt will throw a giant pizza on the roof of his house in a scene so iconic that, to this day, enthusiastic fans will occasionally pelt the roof of the actual location house used in the scene with giant pizzas.

Imagine the pitfalls the writer could have stumbled into as they structured this scene. A couple extra lines of congeniality, a few extra words about eBay, a single question from Skyler – why is Bogdan keeping you so late, honey? – and the scene could have careened into dull irrelevance. For every script every word counts, every line matters, which this work clearly illustrates.

What also counts is the voices of the characters. Past Walt sounds like future Walt but also comes across as more innocent and less stressed than future Walt; the same goes for Skyler. Great dialogue consists of distinct voices for every character that not only service their personas but also the story; in this case, as a comment on how the choices Walt makes in the course of the series will affect his relationship with his wife.

Even the most accessible and simple TV series will offer distinct voices for their key characters. When DC worked on *Diagnosis Murder*, he was well aware that Dick Van Dyke's Doctor Michael Sloan spoke with a distinct cadence and aspect as opposed to the other regular characters. On *Walker, Texas Ranger*, Chuck Norris barely spoke at all. Due to the macho nature of his character and his self-admitted limitations as an actor, Chuck was the only lead DC ever worked with who insisted on giving his lines to other cast members, keeping his dialogue trim, simple and no-nonsense, which perfectly suited the needs of his character and the show. Patrick Stewart, on the other hand, brought years of experience as a talented Shakespearean thespian to his role as Jean-Luc Picard on *Star Trek: the Next Generation*, and DC wrote his dialogue accordingly; rich in vocabulary, syntactic subtlety, and layered education.

Bottom line, if you can't hear a character's voice in your head – if that character can't speak to you in an intriguing or interesting way – then find a fresh approach to the character. Or a new character entirely.

Attitude dialogue

How does one establish character as fast as possible? Through a distinct attitude in their dialogue.

In the case of *As Good As it Gets* (1997), written by Mark Andrus and James L. Brooks, the lead character of Melvin freely uses insults for almost any situation; like when he tells a waitress at his favorite restaurant, "I have Jews at my table."

For the Vulcan character of Spock in the original *Star Trek* series, the character's unemotional response to even the most dramatic situation brought tremendous import to a simply stated, "Fascinating."

And in the classic film noir movie *The Big Sleep* (1946) (screenplay by William Faulkner, Leigh Brackett and Jules Furthman, based on the novel *The Big Sleep* by Raymond Chandler) it's sarcasm.

> CARMEN
> You're not very tall are you?
>
> MARLOWE
> I try to be.

Other than a short exchange of mere introduction with the butler, these are the first words out of private detective Philip Marlowe's mouth and they set the tone of the character and his dealings with everyone else to come in the rest of the movie. Carmen is the general's flirtatious daughter who is being blackmailed because of her misadventures. The film opens with Marlowe arriving at the general's home. After Carmen deliberately falls into his arms before leaving, Marlowe turns to the butler and says, "You should wean her – she's old enough." and later tells the general, "She tried to sit on my lap, while I was standing."

Marlowe's sarcasm is his trademark. It reveals a man who isn't afraid of saying whatever he wants to whomever he wants. He's a straight shooter – at least when it comes to talking. But Marlowe is also a man who has seen a lot of the underbelly of life; his humor has become his way of dealing with it. This makes Marlowe a strong character, a man who treats everyone equally. After he insinuates that the older daughter Vivian is somehow involved with a dangerous gambler named Eddie Mars, she attempts to slap him. But he stops her hand before it even rises and quips, "I don't slap so good this time of the evening."

Marlowe's sarcasm is also a sign of his strength. When Eddie Mars finds him snooping around a dead man's home, Eddie insists Marlowe tell him what job he's working on and for whom. Marlowe refuses, even when Eddie offers to pay him – exhibiting his private eye code of ethics. Then he turns the questioning on Eddie.

> MARLOWE
> How come you had a key?
>
> EDDIE
> Is that any of your business?

> MARLOWE
> I could make it my business.
>
> EDDIE
> And I could make your business my business.
>
> MARLOWE
> You wouldn't like it. The pay's too small.

The lines are lifted almost exactly from Raymond Chandler's novel, which was a smart move on the part of the screenwriters. They were right to retain so much of Chandler's original dialogue here and throughout the screenplay. This particular exchange perfectly sets up the relationship that will continue between Marlowe and Eddie – antagonistic, witty, and sardonic.

Interestingly, Marlowe's sarcasm changes depending on who he is addressing. Sometimes it's hard-nosed, as when he speaks to a thug he gets a drop on and takes away his gun, then pats down another man in the room only to find another gun.

> MARLOWE
> Such a lot of guns around town and so few brains.

But sometimes it has a softer ring of friendship, such as in the beginning of the film when he first meets the general, a man he clearly appreciates.

> GENERAL
> How do you like your brandy, Mr. Marlowe?
>
> MARLOWE
> In a glass.

Here the sarcasm is accompanied with a smile instead of a sneer or a glare. His sarcasm is dismissive towards Carmen, who always flirts with him.

> CARMEN
> Is he as cute as you?
>
> MARLOWE
> (as he forces her out the door) Nobody is.

By the end of the film, Marlowe's sarcasm even begins to rub off on Vivian with whom he falls in love.

> MARLOWE
> What's wrong with you?
>
> VIVIAN
> Nothing you can't fix.

Dialogue that does more than further the plot 37

With this simple switch of who is the straight man and who leads the sarcasm, it is established that their relationship is growing and will become one of equals.

The sarcasm of Philip Marlowe not only flows perpetually throughout the movie, but it became a standard trait for all private eyes to come, a staple of the film noir genre. We can learn a lot from classic films, and especially from film noir.

Period dialogue

Time and place can also have a significant impact on the voices of your characters, the way their scenes are structured, and even the way they look at themselves and the world. In a film like *The Help* (2011) set in the deep South during the worst part of America's post-Civil War apartheid, it would have been hopelessly inappropriate and inaccurate if the project's screenwriter, Tate Taylor, working from a novel by Kathryn Stockett, had allowed the African American characters to be overly familiar with their white employers. For his screenplay for *Lincoln* (2012), Tony Kushner scoured Abraham Lincoln's speeches and writings for the great man's dialogue. Even in a science-fiction piece like *Arrival* (2016), its writer, Eric Heisserer, working from the short story, "Story of Your Life" by Ted Chiang, performed significant research into what form a visual-based alien language could conceivably take.

Writing dialogue for the American western can offer its own special perils. DC co-wrote, with J. Larry Carroll, an episode of a western series, *Lazarus Man* (1996), which focused on the notorious Confederate military prison, Andersonville. He's also written an original screenplay set in southwest Texas during a terrible yellow fever epidemic that tore through the state in 1878. If he had not performed the appropriate research on either project, the stories would have been less than satisfying. But it wasn't simply the dates, facts, or places of the time which required respect and attention; the language needed to be properly suited to the period as well. When it pertains to how people actually talked back then, you'd be surprised at how many traps writers can tumble into while scripting western projects. Many of their common film references or terms were created in Hollywood, not the true west. The term "cowboy" did not exist; the Spanish word "vaquero" was common parlance of the day. There were no "gunfighters," there were "pistoleers" and "shootists." No one said "What the Hell?" as an explanation; "What in the Devil and Tom Walker?" was the usual term.

Needless to say, the average American woman in the mid-19th century west would not comport or express herself like a woman in the early 21st. However, providing a female character with a strong voice in a period project can create a riveting persona while also supporting a believable and captivating story. A superb example of this is the Mattie Ross character as defined in Joel and Ethan Cohn's adaptation of Charles Portis's novel *True Grit* (2010). Like all the people in the book and film, Mattie's dialogue is concise, period-centric, and rich in bitter intention. A good example of this is her last speech in the voice-over that begins the film; a commentary on her father's murder by the coward Tom Chaney in post-Civil War Fort Smith, Arkansas.

> MATTIE
> Chaney fled. He could have taken the time to saddle
> the Horse or hitched up three spans of mules to a
> Concord stagecoach and smoked a pipe, as it seems
> that no one in that city was inclined to give chase.
> Chaney had mistaken its citizens for men.

As Mattie travels to Fort Smith to secure her father's body and pursue his murderer, she enters into or witnesses a series of debates. She hard bargains a horse dealer out of a sizable sum of money, a fresh mount and her father's saddle. She watches a defense lawyer shred Federal Marshal Rooster Cogburn on the stand during a murder trial. She talks Cogburn into pursuing Tom Chaney and ignores bounty hunter LeBoeuf's demands she leave Chaney to him. After the first act, as Mattie forms a team with Cogburn and LeBoeuf while they all pursue Chaney into the lawless Indian Territory, the open debates turn into moments of character, strategy, and conflict. Whatever the scene, all of the people in the story maintain their period-proper cadence and distinct sense of expression, but Mattie, a 14-year-old girl in a world of grown men, violence, and danger, is particularly committed to never losing her aplomb or her sharp tongue.

To LeBoeuf when he introduces himself to her as a Texas Ranger...

> MATTIE
> That may make you a big noise in that state; in Arkansas you
> should mind that your Texas trappings and title do not make
> you an object of fun.

To Cogburn as she hires him to hunt Chaney...

> MATTIE
> Here is the money. I aim to get Tom Chaney and if you are not game
> I will find somebody who is game. All I have heard out of you so far
> is talk. I know you can drink whiskey and snore and spit and
> wallow in filth and bemoan your station. The rest has been
> braggadocio. They told me you had grit and that is why I came to
> you. I am not paying for talk. I can get all the talk I need and
> more at the Monarch Boarding House.

To Ned Pepper after she shoots Tom Chaney – the first time...

> MATTIE
> I will tell you what and you will see that I am in the right. Tom
> Chaney there shot my father to death in Fort Smith and robbed
> him of two gold pieces and stole his mare. Her name is Judy but
> I did not see her down at the river. I was informed Rooster
> Cogburn had grit and I hired him out to find the murderer. A few
> minutes ago I came upon Chaney watering the horses. He would
> not be taken in charge and I shot him. If I had killed him
> I would not be now in this fix. My revolver misfired.

Look at how the dialogue not only moves the story forward but stays true to the period, attitude, and goal of the character. This is no simple accomplishment. Throughout *True Grit*, both the novel and film, the careful attention to proper historical detail is evident in almost every line and vitally important to their success. What made Mattie Ross, an unlikely protagonist for a western, so involving and convincing was the distinct, fresh, and riveting intention of her dialogue. But would this girl have so intrigued and entertained us if her language had consisted of the usual flat and uninspired talk prevalent in so many Westerns?

Another example of a very specific period dialogue style (which also happens to be focused on a strong female lead character) is visible in the pilot for *The Crown* (2016), written by Peter Morgan, when Elizabeth reacts to the news that Anthony Eden has dethroned her trusted prime minister, Winston Churchill.

> ELIZABETH
> Of course one knew it was coming. And
> if one's being frank, there were one
> or two moments where one might even
> hoped for it, too.
>
> CHURCHILL
> Prayed! No doubt!
>
> ELIZABETH
> But now it's come. The emptiness one
> feels – at once. The loneliness. And
> fear. Like a bereavement.

The rhythm and energy of the dialogue is not only true to the characters but also to the time, place, and period. These are very British, very highborn people who deal with crisis and negative circumstance in a particularly British, highborn way. Their point of view must be honored in every scene of every episode no matter the plot, circumstance, or situation. The fact that Elizabeth is a woman prematurely forced into her role as royal liege in 1950s England brings an additional edge and intention to every scene.

Dialogue that reveals character

> "Rick, I have many friends in Casablanca, but because you
> despise me you are the only one I can trust."

Just one great line from one of the best-written dialogue screenplays, *Casablanca* (1942), by Julius J. Epstein, Philip G. Epstein, and Howard Koch, based on an un-produced play *Everyone Comes to Rick's*, written by Murray Burnett and Joan Alison. The film was considered a B-movie at best. Many actors turned down its lead roles and those that did act in the project worked on it strictly under contract. The original two writers, the Epsteins, left the movie before the script was completed and told the producers it was ready to film – leaving Hollywood newcomer Koch to frantically pen pages while shooting was taking place. Some have suggested that the dialogue was so good because of this fast page to stage turnaround, where there wasn't enough time for producers, directors and cast members to mess up what the original writers had created. The screenplay is heavy on talk, but talk sets up character, such as in this early scene with Rick in his bar when he walks past Yvonne, a minor character, downing drink after drink.

> YVONNE
> Where were you last night?
>
> RICK
> That's so long ago, I don't remember.

A pause.

> YVONNE
> Will I see you tonight?
>
> RICK
> I never plan that far ahead.

This is choice dialogue – character-driven, crammed with backstory, which establishes his character quickly and precisely. This man is a loner. He could be a heel to women but the viewer's opinion changes when he gets the drunk Yvonne a cab and orders one of his bartenders to take her home – and come right back. His best frenemy, Renault is forced to comment ...

> RENAULT
> How extravagant you are – throwing away women like that.
> Some day they may be very scarce.

And with this simple line the writers clearly establish the difference between the two friendly adversaries. Renault is someone who takes advantage of people, while Rick is someone who doesn't want to get too involved, but actually cares. Renault's easygoing character is already established at the airport when he greets his superior, the Nazi Major Heinrich Strasser, the true antagonist of the story. Renault, the story's false antagonist, gets to display his own character by telling the major not to worry about picking up the killers of the German couriers, which is why the major has arrived in Casablanca.

> RENAULT
> Oh, there's no hurry. Tonight he'll be at Rick's.
> Everyone comes to Rick's.

From these simple lines we infer that while Strasser is a man all about serious business, Renault is a man all about leisure. He is in no rush to apprehend the killer and he plans to do it over drinks. Just in case we didn't assume that Rick's is a bar, the next shot in the script is the exterior of Rick's Café. But this exchange also sets up how independent Renault is from the Nazis. Major Strasser is his superior, but Renault's calling the shots of what will happen, where and when. This simple exchange helps set up what his character does in the final scene when Rick kills Strasser. When soldiers rush up, instead of turning on Rick, Renault says one of the most famous lines to ever come out of Hollywood: "Round up the usual suspects." We buy this from this character because of the layers of flippant and passive-defiant dialogue the writers have given him.

Some 25 years ago a screenwriter played a trick on the industry and sent the screenplay out under the original title, only changing the character names and with his name as the screenwriter. Every development executive turned it down except for two. One replied, "This would have worked years ago, if it had stars like Humphrey Bogart and Ingrid Berman." The other responded "It's been done before."

Why did so many Hollywood people reject one of the most beloved classical films? First, they felt it was too talky; the screenplay is heavy on talk. But talk sets up character. They also complained about the ending; the hero didn't get the girl. What kind of ending was that? Noble. Something most stories today seem to be lacking in.

Finally they complained that the film needed to be opened up. It took place almost entirely in Rick's Café. Yes there were a few scenes set at the police station, one at another café and one or two at a hotel or in the streets, and the airport – but! *Casablanca* may lack visual expanse and diversity, but because of that, at least in part, it has incredible intimacy.

Who hasn't read the screenplay of *Casablanca* at least once? Many people in Hollywood it would seem. But what *Casablanca* helps to reinforce is the key notion that if the dialogue is truly motivated by the characters (the male characters best demonstrate this with Renault, Rick and Ugarte) it doesn't seem to matter how open the script or how long its scenes may be. If the audience is carried along as the characters' talk moves the story forward and reveals more character then dialogue, the treasure, almost forgotten in today's Hollywood, is perfectly capable of carrying a film. This is something to be remembered, as time goes by.

Poetic dialogue

Sunset Boulevard (1950), by Billy Wilder, Charles Bracket & D. M. Marshman, is the classic Hollywood tragedy. Down and out screenwriter Joe Giles becomes a kept man by forgotten silent film star Norma Desmond. He is sucked into her world of the past, only starting to climb out by writing with and then falling in love with his friend's fiancée. Giles is a user who knows what it's like to be used and finally decides to make a clean break. Norma, falling deeper into her insanity, shoots him as he attempts to walk out on her. The screenplay is included in *Best American Screenplays 3*, edited by Sam Thomas, and is considered a classic of the film noir period because of the darkness in which its characters live and die. The screenplay and film are famous, not only for their portrayal of Hollywood's brutal discarding of those who fall from the spotlight, but for the film's structure and dialogue. *Sunset Boulevard* has one of the most compelling openings of all time, a shot of Giles floating dead in the pool as his voice-over begins.

FLASH OF THE BODY

Angle up through the water from the bottom of the pool, as the body floats face down. It is a well-dressed young man.

> MAN'S VOICE
> You see the body of a young man was found floating in
> the pool of her mansion with two shots in his back
> and one in his stomach. Nobody important, really.
> Just a movie writer, a couple of "B" pictures to his credit.
> The poor dope. He always wanted a pool. Well, in the end
> he got himself a pool – only the price turned out to be a
> little high ... (117)

This is a first-person narrative, and that person is dead. Because he is dead, when the film begins, his hindsight is 20/20. The story could have been told without the narrative voice-overs, but it wouldn't have worked anywhere near as well. The writer's mantra of "show, don't tell" is ignored here and rightfully so, otherwise the picture would have lost its spine, its bite. Giles is not a likable fellow. He is a grumpy, negative, self-pitying loser. Why should we care about him? How could he be a compelling character upon which to hinge a story? It is Joe Giles's inner voice that pushes us to want to know what happened. His sarcastic wit is the hook, his distinct and sparkling brand of cynicism setting the tone for the entire film.

Norma's dialogue perfectly reflects both her ego and her out-of-touch insanity. When Giles says, "You used to be in pictures. You used to be big." Her reply is "I am big. It's the pictures that got small." When she throws him out, Giles quips, "Next time I'll bring my autograph album along, or maybe a hunk of cement and ask for your footprints."

Wilder and company's use of words is priceless. Lines like "She had a voice like a ringmaster's whip" and "Generations of moths had grown fat off that carpet" are as poetic as they are descriptive, while at the same time being true to Giles's voice. These tidbits are insightful to the character, surroundings and action of the film. One of my favorite lines comes at the end, when the cops pull Giles's dead body out of the pool and his voice-over comments, "Funny how gentle people get with you once you're dead."

The film itself is melodramatic at times and its world is dated to its 1950s mores, music and milieu, but the dialogue lives on. While the lines are utilized in voice-over and dialogue, they could just have easily been employed within the descriptive paragraphs to convey the atmosphere and style. It is the poetic phrasing that keeps the film a classic and should inspire any writer to be more creative with their descriptive sentences.

Since 1950, when the film was released, its persistent influence has trickled down throughout Hollywood and the independent film community. Movies like *American Beauty* and even *Memento* owe much to what Wilder and company achieved in *Sunset Boulevard*. Ironically, its famous beginning, which sets the film apart and establishes its tone, was rewritten and reshot after the film was completed and previewed. The original beginning opened with Giles in the morgue having a discussion with other corpses and was seen as laughable by test audiences. Just like *Casablanca*, whose most famous last line, "I think this is the beginning of a beautiful relationship," was thought up on set and *When Harry Met Sally's* most memorable joke, "I'll have what she's having," was thought up in rehearsal by Billy Crystal, so too *Sunset Boulevard*'s famous opening grew out of an organic set of circumstances. Sometimes genius just happens. We need to be open to it when it does, and the way to do that is to not be as cynical as some of the characters we might create.

Contemporary dialogue

It must be mentioned that, unlike period projects such as *True Grit*, when it comes to most modern films, the dialogue is usually spare and to the point; certainly not as rich with the color, description and emotion visible in Mattie Ross's speeches. As in the sample scene from the *Breaking Bad* episode, today's dialogue is carefully designed faux conversation. It's not true, ordinary talk with all the hems and haws, the unnecessary information, introductions and farewells, or sidebars and irrelevancies that appear in the way people normally communicate with each other. Good screen dialogue is specifically chosen and constructed, offering the audience the illusion of an actual conversation while dramatic, structural and character needs are being met.

This is especially true in exposition scenes in genre screenplays with distinct parameters, worlds, and characters – such as murder mysteries and thrillers, science fiction and horror films or crime and heist dramas. All of these films have their own particular style of exposition scenes that lay the basic narrative pipe of their stories – the case presentations in legal thrillers, the exposure of the killer in murder mysteries, crisis meetings in political dramas, and military strategy sessions in war films – that thereby provide the audience with important information.

These scenes are the bane of every screenwriter's existence. If the information is relayed as pure text, just the raw facts, the scene will be as boring as the most lethargic moment in a documentary on Brazilian coffee production. If the scene is too emotional, descriptive or detailed, it can become confusing, unconvincing, or even ludicrous. How does a writer balance the need to relay vital story information while still maintaining dramatic pace and character interest?

For an example of how this can be managed brilliantly, take a look at the key interrogation scene in the heist drama *The Town* (2010), screenplay by Peter Craig, Ben Affleck and Aaron Stockard, based on the novel *Prince of Thieves* by Chuck Hogan. Interrogation scenes are almost impossible to write well; we've seen so many of them and they tend to travel a familiar path: one cop plays bad, another plays good, the suspect resists or surrenders, the cop lies or cajoles. The tension inherent in all these scenes can be immediate, but how do you make it feel interesting or different, truly engrossing as opposed to simply workable?

As the scene in *The Town* begins, Dino, a Federal officer, welcomes Doug, Ben Affleck's character, a notorious bank robber and the ostensible hero of the film, into the interrogation room. The two men begin with an exchange about Doug's father with Dino mentioning that he sent him to prison and that he knows the old man just got hurt up there. As Doug is dealing with this, Dino tries to throw him a curve, saying "You know we pulled a print off the van, right?" Namely the van that Doug's gang used in their last robbery.

This is when Dino's boss Frawley enters and launches into a speech that not only serves the scene but also offers a bitter commentary on every interrogation we've ever witnessed in every crime drama. He tells Doug that in the Academy he was taught . . .

>
> FRAWLEY
> During interrogations, always begin treating the subject kindly so as to win his trust, the logic being that you can always turn ugly later but it's very difficult to start off unsympathetic and later become what we call a "trusted figure."

Frawley then reverses course, telling Doug that he's an asshole and he's not going to do what he was trained to do at all. Doug and his gang simply have gone too far, as Frawley colorfully explains. . .

>
> FRAWLEY
> You didn't just roll a Star Market in Malden for a box of quarters. You banged it out in the North End with assault rifles at nine in the morning. You fucked yourself, right in the mouth. Because if the 7.62 rounds weren't enough to smear you with the scent of fetid meat and attract every slophound law enforcement from here to Springfield – you fucking dummies shot a guard. Now you're like a half-off sale at Big and Tall: every cop is in line. However, this guard, who is two-thirds to a retard, has miraculously clung to life. If they gave me two minutes and a wet towel, I would personally asphyxiate that half-wit so we could string you up for Federal M1 and end this story with a bag on your head and a paralyzing agent running through your veins.

Dialogue that does more than further the plot 45

As Doug continues to listen silently, Frawley lowers the boom...

>   FRAWLEY
> You're here today so I could tell you personally that
> you're going to die in Federal prison. And so are all your
> friends. No deal. No compromise. And when that day comes,
> when you start trying to be my hero collaborator so hard
> I have to slap you to shut up - and it will - despite your
> pitiable, misguided, Irish "Omerta" - when your "code of
> silence" gives way to the fear of trafficking in cigarettes
> to prevent sexual enslavement - I just want you to know,
> it's gonna be me who tells you to go fuck yourself.

At this point, the writer could have fallen into a variety of lethal traps – such as having Doug get angry and deny or simply insult and evade. Instead the writer made an interesting and fresh choice; he has Doug attack the FBI's surveillance techniques, revealing he and his guys were fully aware when – earlier in the story – Frawley's men were watching his team enjoy a barbecue in Charlestown.

>   DOUG
> Next time you want to take pictures of me and my friends,
> could we do a calendar shoot? Maybe lubed up on a tire or
> something?

This is the first time Dino and Frawley realize they were made on their surveillance.

>   DOUG
> Your antennas are the flat half-inch matte black. Statie
> are pigtailed and BPD half and half. Every peewee in the
> Town knows what a Feebie rear antenna looks like. So in
> the future, if you're gonna try to be slick - be slicker
> than a ten-year-old.
>   (puts on coat)
> Good luck with the print.

With that, Doug is out the door and the scene is over. Not only have the usual parameters of the interrogation scene been turned on their head from both directions – the interrogator and the interrogated – we have a fresh, dramatic and telling moment. We see two distinct and extremely colorful voices offer a captivating pair of adversaries. We also receive vital information – how much Frawley and his men know, and how much Doug knows about what they know – in an unexpected and entertaining fashion.

Take note of the dialogue's location-centric color – "a Star Market in Malden" – and crime-orientated nomenclature – "Your antennas are the flat half-inch matte black." No matter where your story is set or who the characters are their dialogue should reflect some specifics about their surroundings, class, or place in time and period.

Even a simple and utterly accessible detail like the vehicle a character drives can offer significant emotional definition or help maintain audience interest. Don't have your hero complain about his truck having a flat tire – his Ford 150 blew a custom steel rim. Your heroine's new hairdo wasn't simply spoiled in the rain – the up and down curly bob she just got at Sally Anne's Texture Salon was ruined. A child didn't lose a toy – the Boogie Man stole their new Tri Fidget Spinner. Keep track of your character's world in his or her dialogue, and the audience will more likely keep track of their story.

When talk is action

Nora Ephron's wonderful screenplay for *When Harry Met Sally* (1989) has absolutely no action. That's a bold step to take, especially in modern-day Hollywood. Of course, she was working with director Rob Reiner, from whose films one might surmise that he believes that talk is action. *Stand by Me*, *The American President*, *A Few Good Men*, and even *Misery* are movies full of talk. Nora Ephron is a kindred spirit, evident from her screenplays for *You've Got Mail*, *Sleepless in Seattle*, *Michael*, *My Blue Heaven*, and of course, what is arguably her best work, *When Harry Met Sally*.

Someone, actually many people, has said that movies are action. True. But action can come in many forms. Conflict is action and conflict does not have to be physical violence, battles in space or sweeping treks across scenic horizons. Conflict can, and often does, come from character, and character is revealed best through dialogue. Thus, there are times when talk is action. Action/talk is dialogue that progresses not only the character and plot, but presents conflict.

Exploring an age-old question, Harry and Sally disagree over whether a man and a woman can be friends without sex entering into the equation. Thus Ephron sets up a battle of the sexes through thoughts and words, and, best of all, she flavors the talk with humor and insight. When people go out on a date or to a party they talk. Talking is their recreation as well as communication. It is also exploration and often insightful. Action without talk is visual, and certainly characterization can be conveyed with glances, gestures, reactions or lack thereof. But talk is a universal human instinct and need. Why do we talk to ourselves, sing in the shower or repeat our favorite lines from the movies? Verbal communication is something that can be done best within the dramatic arts. Movies allow us not only the expanse of time and place, they enable us to fulfill our voyeuristic tendencies, one of the biggest being eavesdropping.

Of course, the trick to all good-talk screenplays is writing clever, engaging dialogue and not boring the audience with trite, clichéd or uninteresting realism. Harry and Sally come across as authentic, appealing people, due to how they talk. This is Ephron's art, for her dialogue is nowhere close to real. People, in reality, are never nearly this clever, witty and open. Harry and

Sally talk about everything and anything – without fear or embarrassment – and then counter each other without fear of offending or rejection. This is every human's ideal relationship – a totally open avenue of communication where two people can truly be themselves and not be punished, or afraid, or hurt, or hurt someone else.

While this could be what made *When Harry Met Sally* such a universal success, if we look even deeper, we can see it is the sharing between the sexes of their outlooks on life and relationships that made the film so involving. Sally is far from a weak individual; this is a strong woman who more than holds her own with Harry. However, at the same time, her vulnerabilities, needs and desires are also exposed and explored. The same can be said for the Harry character. As the story progresses, the mysteries of how the other half thinks are revealed with humor and simplicity. As in this scene ...

>   HARRY
> That's it? A faceless guy rips off your clothes. And
> that's the sex fantasy you've been having since you were
> twelve? Exactly the same?
>
>   SALLY
> Well, sometimes I vary it a little.
>
>   HARRY
> Which part?
>
>   SALLY
> What I'm wearing.
>
> Harry reacts.
>
>   SALLY
> WHAT?
>
>   HARRY
> Nothing.

Great stuff – great talk. It's better than unbelievable action any day. Ephron's talk is all the action needed in *When Harry Met Sally*, which is one of the main reasons she'll be sorely missed by all who love movies. But her legacy and her talent should be an inspiration for us all.

To sum up, great dialogue offers a rich variety of approaches and styles: from the simple and colorful to the immediate and subtle. In every case examined here, the writer(s) took intense care to do their research on their characters, their world, and their situation, and then just as carefully chose the words that would come out of their mouths and speak their lives to the audience.

What did we learn?

Talk is action.

Great talk has attitude, at least for the right characters.

Every distinctive and well-developed television character has an established voice, and it's the television writer's job to become a chameleon, recreating that voice in their own scripts for any particular show.

If your talk is procedural in regards to a specific profession or world, then you must do your research and know your stuff.

If your talk takes place in a particular period, time and/or place, then you must do your research and know your stuff.

Watch classic films. It doesn't matter how old they are; their talk can still apply to what you're writing today.

Exercise

For this exercise you will write three scenes all set in the same generic location – a bar, restaurant, apartment, etc. Each scene will occur between two people who are in a romantic relationship and are at odds with each other. Every scene will be focused on these same two characters. If you happen to have a scene appropriate to this exercise in your current project, that's all to the better.

In the first scene, we're in a comedy.
In the second, it's an intense drama.
In the third scene, write it as a period piece.

Use the same people and location but set it in some part of past history which will require some research to the pattern of the dialogue and the attitudes of the character suitable to that period. If you really want to get creative, set the scene in the future or on a distant planet – so long as it's the same two people in a similar location – and invent character attitudes and dialogue patterns that you feel would be suitable to that future or alien time or place.

Now do all three scenes again, only reverse the sexes, or at least the attitudes, of your characters and their circumstance; building a fresh angle on every scene. This exercise should give you at least some idea of how many amazing and unexpected ways you can approach a single moment between two characters.

5 Poetic description

This may be an absurdly obvious point, but screenwriters, whatever their level or experience, need to read screenplays. A script's format, while deceptively simple, is challenging in its specific and unique demands. Screenplays are written for two audiences: the Hollywood script reader first, the movie viewing audience second. If a screenplay is not written to proper format then the readers at competitions, agencies, and production companies will reject the finished product almost out of hand. This is particularly true when it comes to writing description – or the "action" lines as most screenwriting programs describe them. This is the material that literally describes the visuals, environment, character details or action in every scene. Even when a writer creates solid dialogue to support a well-defined plot and characters, if the glue that holds it altogether, the action lines, the description, is over or under written, confusing or misleading, the entire project will never get past those readers, let alone get produced.

Books and seminars are filled to the brim with "rules" on how to write a screenplay. One of the biggest is not to write poetically but conserve your words. Beginning scripters start out writing too much detail and often with too poetic or detailed a style. Screenplays only have 90–120 pages. The popular script gurus say be short and direct with everything you write, not only in your dialogue but your imagery. The action must be as specific and engaging as possible but also strong and dramatic enough to pull the reader into the story in each given moment in an immediate, even visceral way. Most important of all, you must tell the reader what he or she is SEEING. At the top of every scene, after every slug or setting line, the action must be established with some kind of visual image – even if it's as simple as explaining who is in the scene and what they are doing.

Choosing your words

The riveting appearance of the first zombie in the pilot for *The Walking Dead* (2010–) television series – written by Frank Darabont, based on the graphic novel by Robert Kirkland – is a superb case in point. In this moment, police officer Rick Grimes, the show's point-of-view hero, spots what he thinks is a lost little girl wandering by a highway and rushes to help her. But when he catches up with the child . . .

```
She turns. Staring at him with deep, sunken eyes/flesh drawn
tight on skull and bone. Lips torn away, leaving just a snarl
of teeth. She's got braces. Clots of old decayed meat caught
in the metal.

She's dead.

Not sick. Not dressed up for Halloween. Dead.
```

Not a lot of words here but what we read is choice – extremely dramatic and immediate. Every bit of description has energy and impact, even a deep sense of sorrow. This is simple and effective yet still emotional. All communication in art is through emotion, and the art form of the screenplay is no different. Whether the feeling is grief, tension, excitement, or even simple ironic fun, the script must carry that feeling through every sentence of its description – which in turn connects the dialogue, plot, and theme of the piece together into one elaborate and fascinating puzzle. The key is to employ strong and visual language as efficiently as possible. The fewer words the better; less is more. This is clear in another example – the introduction of the pivotal character of Ned Stark in the pilot episode of *Game of Thrones* (2011–).

```
LORD EDDARD "NED" STARK (40) sits on his motionless horse, his
long brown hair stirring in the wind. His closely trimmed
beard is shot with white. He has spent half his life training
for war and the other half waging it, and his face conveys both
authority and a haunted sadness.
```

Not a lot of words but what's been used clearly relates a character history that supports the story and the plot but provides practical specifics in casting. Again, a script not only serves as a dramatic engine, it's a blueprint for every aspect of production, including who plays a particular role in any given scene as well as that scene's location, props, and costuming.

In the case of today's action films, where there is so much visual information, the writing can be intense, even primal, serving dramatic and filmic needs as well as establishing production parameters. A basic and simple way to write action is to look on each line of description as a visual moment or shot. The horror film *Annabelle* (2014), written by Gary Dauberman, offers a typical example.

```
John BURSTS through the bedroom door.

Tackles the Man.

Knife falls.

Skids across the floor.
```

Mia collapses.

Blood soaks her nightgown.

She looks over at –

John and the Man wrestling on the floor. John pins the Man down with his knees and –

POUNDS-POUNDS-POUNDS his face in with his fists when –

The Woman – YELLING LIKE A BANSHEE – enters and LEAPS onto John's BACK. Sinks her teeth in his shoulder. A rabid dog.

The opening scene of *Deadpool* (2016) – written by Rhett Reese & Paul Wernick – is supremely successful in establishing the world and title character of a wild, intense comic book action project.

DEADPOOL, in full DRESS REDS and MASK, quietly FIDGETS in the BACK SEAT of a TAXI CAB as it proceeds along a CITY FREEWAY.

Deadpool adjusts the two KATANAS strapped to his back. Rolls the WINDOWS up, down, up. Tries futilely to untwist the seatbelt, then LUNGES forward, locking it up. Rifles through a tourist booklet and tears out a HAUNTED SEGWAY TOUR coupon. The CABBIE, young, thin, brown, glances back and forth from the rear view to the road to the rear view.

In short order, the tone of the film is established – colorful but succinct, energetic and quick, irreverent yet focused. This is an approach that is quite specific in its detail with a general intention that is fun and silly yet somehow sincere. We get the strong message that this project and its lead character will not take themselves seriously, that this movie will be a carnival ride. But despite the over-the-top tomfoolery, careful attention has been paid to the details in location, props, attire, and character. Since this is a production draft, key elements are capped to facilitate the work of the department heads. As a general rule in the writing of speculative screenplays, capping props, action, sounds, and music cues should be kept to a minimum for the sake of basic readability. However, the energy and style displayed here is an approach writers should consider emulating, at least for an action or action-comedy project.

Describing for the mind's eye

Alan Ball, in his award-winning screenplay *American Beauty* (1999), has proven that one can employ poetic description that is short and moves the reader to "see" the movie.

```
Ricky is 18, but his eyes are much older. Beneath his zen-like
tranquility lurks something wounded... and dangerous.
```

We know many writers who would say to cut this – "write only what you can show" they would recite, but Ball here gives the actor and the reader something to hang the character on. Can it be shown on screen? If the director and actor are good enough, of course. But even more so, it speaks directly to the reader of the screenplay, allowing them to enjoy the read.

```
She smiles her most winning smile at him. He knows this persona
well, only it's never pissed him off as much as it does
right now.
```

Ball could have written "She smiles. He frowns," which is what some books and seminars would recommend. But Ball knows that, without capturing the reader's attention and interest, the script will never be passed along. Yes, the story is strong, but the writing is what keeps the reader turning the page. Entertain the reader first, which Ball does so well. He never goes overboard with the "fiction" elements, adding just enough to both illustrate and give image to the screen story.

```
They look at each other for a beat, then look away. This situ-
ation is loaded and they know it.
```

Again, a line you'd expect more in fiction than in a screenplay. There are so many of these, and they are refreshing and often clever.

```
He smiles, then opens his menu. Carolyn picks hers up mechanic-
ally, but continues to stare at him, enraptured, like a fervent
Christian who's just come face to face with Jesus.
```

How does this speak to us as writers? Perhaps we've allowed ourselves to be taken in too much by the "write only what can be shown" rule. The answer isn't to write a screenplay like a book either. There is a middle ground: concise, but poetic, a judicious use of simile, a smart use of color, description and metaphor. All writers have been guilty of too many lines between the dialogue, and more often too much dialogue. Then we go to the other extreme. A writer must find a middle ground. Ball has mastered it and sets a good example for the rest of us. But let's look at another specimen.

Writing for the reader

Big Fish (2003), screenplay by John August, based on the book, *Big Fish: A Novel of Mythic Proportions* by Daniel Wallace, is exactly what its title says it is – a big fish story. It is a tale of modern myths told in a mythical style. August isn't shy about writing in his descriptions little asides to the reader, such as "Is this guy crazy?" and wonderful metaphoric phrases such as "He's the legless cricket left on the anthill." As a matter of fact, barely a page goes by without them.

All of these could easily be cut. It would no doubt lower the page count significantly under the 122 pages it is now. And that is the standard advice from most screenwriting books and seminars that preach, "Save it for your novel." They want a lean, clean and concise screenplay. No extra words, no flowery writing. That certainly is a good advice for the beginning writer, who has a tendency to write a screenplay like a short story or a book with too much description and prose that can't be shown on the screen. But August is writing a story that virtually requires the flippant style he uses in his screenplay. *Big Fish* is a simple story about a father and son who don't really connect, but this is positioned almost as the subplot. The main plot is the collection of big fish tales the father recites year after year, and the underlying question: how much of myth is based on truth?

Flashback within flashback, tons of voice-over narration and a conversational writing style makes the screenplay *Big Fish* a captivating read. David Landau's (DL) 12-year-old daughter, who never saw the film, read it from cover to cover and loved it. Now, we're not trying to imply that studio executives have the mentality of a 12 year old (after all, DL's daughter is witty and creative). But if August's writing can connect with her then it certainly can connect with a script reader, a development exec., a film producer, a screenplay contest judge, an agent, a director, an actor or any other sort of person who reads scripts.

Each of August's little asides and turned phrases speaks volumes. They set the tone, not only in the reader's mind but for the director, the cast and crew.

```
She looks like she's been dead for years, but too stubborn to lie down.
```

```
And in the silence that follows, a lot is said. It wasn't the upbeat reply Sandra was hoping for.
```

```
And that's the sad truth. Karl is less a monster that a freak – a giant man, but in the end, just a man.
```

```
ON EDWARD as his heart falls 20 floors.
```

Each of these could be cut or simplified into clean clear stage directions and descriptions. But that wouldn't be right for this screenplay. Why? Because this is a film of epic lies which are told with a nod and wink. The screenplay must be written with the same nods and winks that the main character uses to spin his tales. It is a matter of tone, not just setting. It is also a matter of good writing. Good writing makes good reading, and good reading makes good films. Because a lot of people will be working to make that script into a finished film, they all must have the same image in their mind, giving them a good handle on the tone and the style of the project.

Would this approach work for a suspense-thriller? Probably not; it would be the wrong quality or tone. A dark tense story would seem to cry out for short, precise description not dissimilar to the approach used in the action scene from *Annabelle* – almost a staccato style that would better match the feeling of the movie. *Big Fish* is a lyrical film and thus its lyrical language is not just justified, but demanded.

When writing, we have to do more than stay aware of the tone of our story. The fashion in which we choose to write it can be a great device in communicating and maintaining that project's basic emotional approach to any and all who may pick up the pages. So we as writers should carefully select the technique in which we tell our tales on paper. The style of the screenplay can imply the style of the finished film. Making a conscious choice and making it work is one of the differences between being an artist and being a craftsman.

Humorously said

And let's finish this chapter with a film we've talked about a great deal in this book. Ted Elliot & Terry Rossio's screenplay for the hit film *Pirates of the Caribbean: The Curse of the Black Pearl* (2003) which crosses genres and challenges convention. Most people wouldn't think a pirate, adventure/romantic comedy/supernatural horror film would work, much less attempt writing one. One of the things that stands out about Elliot and Rossio's screenplay is how they utilized humor within the writing style of the script to establish the tone and allow the reader to experience the funhouse ride they wanted the film to become. The screenplay we've read was an early draft and several changes were made before the final shooting script, but, in a way, it is the earliest draft that is the most important, as it is the first one that any readers experienced.

Beginning on page one, the writers use clever word play to describe their characters. "JOSHAMEE GIBBS, who was born old," and "NORRINGTON, a dashing young man, Royal Navy to the core," demonstrate a flair for using words to convey images and character with fast, off-the-cuff comments. They demonstrate a masterful grasp of short, visually descriptive and poetic writing. In this fashion, Elliot and Rossio draw the reader into the movie they see in their heads throughout the script. Phrases such as, "He polishes the toes of his boots on the back of his calves, but it doesn't help," and "He has no choice – and it pisses him off," paint character and action with the humorous touch the writers want to establish as the tone of their story.

"Elizabeth stands on the stairs. Granted, the dress may be painful to wear, but holy smokes!" In the actual movie, the dress is nothing exceptional. But Elliot and Rossio are writing for two audiences – the script reader first, the movie viewing audience second. By using humorous asides and offhand remarks, the writers make the script a fun read and thus a fun movie in the mind of the reader. Which gets it recommended to any other potential readers. Which is then a fun read for the producers, the director, the actors, the art director, and the costume designer, etc. Because of the style in which they wrote their description, everyone involved in the project is working from the same page, as the saying goes.

Writing for the reader rather than the end movie viewer is not a new or unusual concept within screenwriting, but Elliot and Rossio go further out on a limb than most books or screenwriting seminars would ever recommend. They don't even introduce the story's true antagonist, Barbossa, the mutinous captain of the *Black Pearl*, until page 44, and they do it with, "Despite the bright colors of clothing, definitely not a man you'd want to meet in a dark alley – or anywhere, for that matter." The writers could have just written "A dangerous pirate" and be done with it, but they didn't. Throughout the screenplay Elliot and Rossio take the risk of adding "unnecessary" words and sentences, most often sharp and charming ones, to help convey the overall clever tone of the piece.

```
We follow Elizabeth amid foam and bubbles as she PLUNGES down
though the water. Blue and clear, with streaks of sunlight cut-
ting down: bright coral and tropical fish, and a lovely young woman
in a silk dress ... if it weren't for the mortal danger, the scene
could be described as gorgeous.
```

Screenwriting books and seminars always hammer in "less is more" and "save it for your novel" when criticizing a writer who doesn't make each sentence as succinct as possible. Adhering too close to this process risks the loss of the writer's personal style. While that may be fine for a shooting script, it won't help the initial story get sold. Hollywood readers are literally inundated with hundreds of scripts. A dry fast read will not leave as lasting a memory in this poor overworked reader's mind as much as a longer but much more entertaining experience. The unique writer's voice is best on display not in the overall story, but in how they write their descriptions – the words of action they choose to put on paper. A script that is enjoyable to read is much easier to recommend and succeeds better in delivering the mental images of what the writer wishes his story to look like on the screen. This is what Elliot & Rossio achieved so well in their screenplay for *Pirates of the Caribbean: The Curse of the Black Pearl*. You can do it too.

What did we learn?

Choose your words carefully. Be specific in your description.
Depending on the story or the situation, you can embroider and color your description beyond the basic needs of communication and production.
Write for production second, the reader first, otherwise your script will never get into production.
Humor can be your best weapon selling your description.
And read, read, read, read produced screenplays; as many as you can get your hands on.

Exercise

The first, key step to writing good description is in defining the location or world of a particular scene. Choose a real-life location – home, school, place of business, restaurant, or sports venue – within which you have experienced a strong emotional moment or connection. Create two dramatic scenes – one based in that location's exterior and one in its interior – which will be focused on the same two individuals. These characters should at least resemble people you know so you may best be able to describe them as well as the location.

As you write your scenes, "milk" the location in the sense that your characters are doing something visual and dramatic within it – arguing or talking while painting a house, playing a game in a backyard, making love in a bathroom, drowning in a pool, cooking in a kitchen, etc. The focus of the scene should be on how your characters interact within this environment and how you describe that interaction.

Once you finish the two dramatic scenes, pick a new location and write two comic scenes. Then do two pure action scenes in another location, interior and exterior. But whatever the genre or approach of the scene, focus on your characters: always the same two people.

The point of this exercise is to describe a world you can clearly SEE so well that anyone can see it as well as you can. Writing these scenes should help you show a reader the world of your characters and how they live, work, play, or suffer in it.

As you create these passages, manage them with different styles. In one, limit the word count, using the succinct, less-is-more attitude employed in most screenplays. In others, try a colorful, ironic slant à la *Big Fish*, the fun, wry tactics of *Pirates of the Caribbean*, or even *Deadpool*'s comic book approach. Take some chances and push the envelope, writing at least one scene in an evocative form you're not familiar or even comfortable with. In this manner you can get a feel for a variety of descriptive styles while also gaining some valuable experience in making your reader SEE.

6 Finding the theme

To quote from Wikipedia,

> **a theme**, from Old French tesme, is a broad idea in a story or literary work, or a message or lesson conveyed by a written text. This message is usually about life, society, or human nature. Themes often explore timeless and universal ideas. Most themes are implied rather than explicitly stated. The theme is different from the superficial outlay of the text; it is normally the meaning of the text on a deeper, more abstract level.

Themes are not some fancy superstructure attached to only the most carefully wrought and significant films. Every tale, whatever its format, be it a screenplay, a short story, a cave painting or an advertisement for soap, offers a theme. It can be primitive and direct as in the coda of revenge motivating *Rambo*, or complex and rich, as in the notions of greed and misplaced justice that underlay *No Country for Old Men*, but there will always be a theme. Even the Three Stooges shorts produced in the 1930s and 1940s offered a theme, one that repeatedly and farcically dramatized that there were three particular adult humans in this world who could be more foolish, self-destructive and absurd than any child alive (no doubt an attractive concept to a children's audience.)

Popular movies have themes

Pirates of the Caribbean: The Curse of the Black Pearl (2003), is a wonderful example of a well-made, well-written Hollywood action film with a strong, recognizable and accessible theme. The plot is ingenious, the setting fascinating, the characters well defined, and its foundation a mix of unusual genres that still function well together. If the writers of more so-called mainstream character driven dramas paid as close attention to craft as the authors of this project, their stories would be far more successful and satisfying.

The theme of *Pirates* is almost entirely focused on the value of freedom while still reckoning with its consequences. The central message of the film could be defined as: be careful what you wish for, but then pursue that desire with everything you've got. It's extremely rare for a Hollywood, mainstream, popcorn, tent-pole project to so ably and richly illustrate such an important and human idea in such an entertaining fashion. Employing fascinatingly designed and well-played characters within a carefully structured, period appropriate, and fresh plotline, while still taking the best advantage of many familiar pirate film tropes and set pieces, the first *Pirates of the Caribbean* is a film that not only succeeds as entertainment but as a satisfying comment on the necessity and responsibility of human freedom.

The movie begins as a dream with a little girl standing on a ship in the mist at sea, wishing to meet a pirate. Almost immediately she meets her pirate and her journey, along with the audience's, is launched. For Elizabeth, our point-of-view character, pirates and piracy equal adventure, freedom and romance, all of which she eventually encounters in the course of the story. She also faces great danger, painful disappointment, and threats to her life and freedom. But through unalloyed courage, tenacity and intelligence she eventually achieves her goal, a potential object lesson for even women of today.

The central conflict of *Pirates* is the battle between total repression and utter freedom, which also mirrors the film's basic theme. In Elizabeth's world, she lives in sunlight and comfort, surrounded by servants and luxury, but she's a prisoner. Her father brings her a dress that suffocates the girl, Norrington literally compares her to an object as he proposes marriage to her, and everyone, as Swann and Norrington continually remind us, must know their place. Will is so aware of these societal restraints; he can't even bring himself to call the woman he loves by her first name. It's telling that when the pirates arrive at Port Royale, the only truly free person in town, Jack Sparrow, is in jail.

The pirates, on the other hand, represent the other extreme. They are freedom unfettered. They kill, destroy, and loot without restraint. They are nightmare creatures that bring darkness and destruction with them. Whenever we are with the pirates, we live in mist, night, or shadow. Their unvarnished appetites have earned them a curse that has turned them into undead ghouls, and their only desire is to rid themselves of this affliction so they may enjoy the fruits of their piratical depredations.

The war between these forces, between darkness and light, freedom and repression, cruelty and kindness, morality and immorality, defines every scene in the film while also supporting its central theme. This informs the story with a depth of feeling unusual for a project like this, yet it's still accessible and fairly simple.

The script isn't burdened with overblown explanations of this dichotomy, outside of a few key speeches, so the story plays out like an ordinary action adventure film. But it's more than that, and the audience, whether they're aware of it or not, has clearly responded to it.

Shared themes of westerns and horror

Sometimes the world of a film dovetails, enhances, or focuses a film's theme. For example, an environment defined by isolation on a rough frontier restrained in space, population and time will provide solid dramatic support for the common themes of brutal characters, justice, and retribution of a western film. Establishing a limited, untrustworthy civilization can enhance the basic theme of chaos and evil battling against justice and decency that is at the heart of most westerns. In these films, the world is in disorder or threatened with disorder, and only the hero can bring peace to a society in such disarray.

The theme of order against disorder also applies to almost all horror films. Unlike western protagonists such as Mattie Ross in *True Grit* (2010) who successfully hunts down Tom Chaney, the man who murdered her father, the hero rarely brings any true balance to the malevolent little universe of most horror movies. In these films, total madness and evil have usually seized the world, or the world of the story, and the protagonist's eventual partial triumph over these forces can be quite satisfying to an audience that may feel they lack control over their own lives and environments. If Ripley can defeat an army of extraterrestrial monsters and their queen practically single-handed in *Aliens*, then a heavy mortgage, prohibitively expensive medical insurance or an IRS audit will not conquer the rest of us.

We have met the enemy and they are us

The key difference between the themes of many western and horror films is in the nature of its central threat. While Tom Chaney in *True Grit* is clearly a dangerous man, he is still fundamentally human in his actions and impulses. The villains in horror films are often a representation of demons or the Devil: pitiless monsters impossible to, as the character Reese says so memorably in *The Terminator*, "be reasoned with. It can't be bargained with … it doesn't feel pity or remorse or fear … and it absolutely will not stop. Ever. Until you are dead."

Even in a horror film like *Don't Breathe* where there are no inhuman "monsters" in the classic sense, the blind antagonist has basically lost his humanity and become a fiend capable of slaughtering anyone to achieve his twisted goals. Disorder coupled with the Devil in a confined environment can create an almost unbearable sense of tension and jeopardy.

Again, the theme is substantial, one that is identifiable to all of us in this current, apparently deranged age. What modern citizen is not concerned that civilization is headed for total collapse whether through climate change, political lunacy, or international aggression? The greatest danger we all fear – our fellow man gone mad – is powerfully dramatized in television's *The Walking Dead*. Those bloodthirsty zombies are not just animated corpses; they represent "the other," the people that will come to destroy us in our schools, businesses and homes – whether they are gang members, foreign terrorists, or white supremacists. We all fundamentally know there is no greater danger to man in the modern world than man, which is why, even when a film's villains are vampires, aliens, or swamp monsters; they still represent some malignant aspect of the Devil ready to burst out from inside all of us.

The stronger the theme, the stronger the story

Putting aside issues of execution and craftsmanship, which, if poorly handled, can defeat any project's themes, no matter how profound (witness the overdone and unsatisfying *Cold Mountain*), the stronger its theme, the stronger the film. The more complex and involving a project's intentions in exploring life, society, and/or human nature, the more satisfying and involving an experience it can offer its audience. When a feature film project with a fascinating setting and strong characters is matched with a substantial theme, the examination of the conflicts available in societal, economic, and ethnic issues inherent to such a concept can be profound in its implications in both a dramatic and political sense.

A classic case in point is the modern western, *The Three Burials of Melquideas Estrada* (2005). If ever a film's themes focused on life, society, and human nature in a dramatic construct to a superlative and sublime result, it's this one. As the landscape and culture of the Rio Grande Valley can clash, confuse and fascinate, so do the people and places of *The Three Burials of Melquideas Estrada*. Despite the challenging structure of Guillermo Arriaga's screenplay, similar in its brazen manipulation in time and harsh circumstance to the same writer's *21 Grams, Babel* and *Amores Perros*, this film is ostensibly, at least in its basic premise, a simple murder mystery. When the body of Meliquideas Estrada, ranch hand and illegal immigrant, is found buried in the desert near the Texas–Mexican border, his boss and best friend, Pete Perkins, is determined to exact a proper justice. He tracks down the killer – Mike Norton, a brutish Border Patrol agent who carelessly shot Melquideas when the man interrupted his personal encounter in the desert with an issue of *Hustler* – and kidnaps him. Pete forces Norton to dig up Melquideas's body, which has been transferred to a potter's plot, then sets off on an epic journey across the rugged border to Mexico to return his friend to his family and a proper burial, or the third burial of the title.

At this point, the film moves beyond simple western revenge-plot mechanics into realms both metaphysical and emotional. Our expectations and even our basic understanding of the characters and their situation are confounded. Pete soon learns that the halcyon life, family and town Melquideas had so glowingly described to him never existed. The ostensible hero of this piece has sacrificed everything that mattered to him, his home, job, and, we can suppose, his freedom, for a lie.

At the same time, Mike Norton, the man Pete has tortured and abused throughout the journey, a beast prone to raping his wife in their kitchen in-between picking his toes, recovers the most precious thing a man can lose: his soul. Norton's final line, "Are you going to be alright?" offered to the man who has kidnapped, tortured, and threatened him, is a revelation that informs the audience, powerfully and dramatically, that even the most inhuman of us can change in the most profound sense, rediscovering their basic humanity, while the best of us can lose theirs even with the best of intentions.

That this tale takes place between two distinct cultures clashing and interweaving across a harsh, beautiful, and demanding landscape only enhances its themes. For when all is said and done in this film, the basic message is that what defines us as people, whether Mexican or American, strong or weak, decent or indecent, is how deeply and how honestly we can feel for others, no matter the world we inhabit. Pete's love for Melquideas Estrada destroys him because it was built on lies and self-deception; both his own and his friend's. Norton, ironically, is saved because, until he encounters Pete, he possesses no heart, empathy or regard for anyone, but he also has no established principals to direct or mislead him. Norton is a child in need of parenting and Pete becomes the man's father, leading by example, if a harsh one. That Pete can offer Norton such an amazing gift, even unintentionally, transforms *The Three Burials of Melquideas Estrada* into a unique and fascinating comment on the human condition.

What more could you ask for in a film's theme? What more could you ask for in a well-written screenplay?

Even comedy has a theme

What makes some comedies stand the test of time while others fade as fast as the news in *Daily Variety*? Theme. The authors of this work can honestly say we've never had a development person or a producer ask us what the theme of any of our work is. But it's there all the same. If it wasn't, they probably wouldn't get past page five or even ask to read it. Theme can be even more important in a comedy than in a drama. Elaine May's screenplay for *The Birdcage* (1996) is a perfect example.

While the original story is by Jean Poiret, May modernized not only its time and place, but its prejudices and humor, and with that, its theme. Rather than a comedy devoted to only silly fun, May's *The Birdcage* literally sings its theme in the opening credits: "We are family." This is a story about commitment, love and family, and what people will put themselves through to achieve them. This may sound like *Romeo and Juliet*, but *The Birdcage* isn't a tragedy. It's one of the funniest movies ever produced. As its story begins, we meet a young man, Val, and his father, Armand, who owns the transvestite nightclub The Birdcage and is in a lifelong relationship with its lead singer, Albert. They raised him. But Val wants to marry the daughter of a conservative politician running for re-election on family morals. Would it be funny if the film were just about drag queens and a conservative politician? Sure. But would it be a lasting comedy? Probably not.

While the original *La Cage aux Folles* is a bit over the top, May strived to not let that happen in her screenplay. Yes, there were eccentric fun characters, like Albert and the houseboy Agador, but they were written as real people with identifiable feelings and desires. May added the subplot that Albert wants a palimony agreement with Armand. This becomes his goal – a formal commitment from his lifelong love and partner. Isn't this something we can all identify with? By adding this undercurrent, the comedy is driven home while the stakes are raised substantially.

Val's goal and intentions are clear, but these change by the end of the story when he finally admits that Albert is his mother and not his biological mother who has arrived late for the dinner. He learns there is nothing to be ashamed of when you truly, deeply love someone. They are part of your family.

Yes, it is a rather standard plot ploy to show that the unorthodox family is closer and more loving than the traditional conservative family. But May makes it work with great moments, delivered to perfection by the great cast, as when the over-the-top Albert dresses in a severe dark suit to meet the potential in-laws.

                    ALBERT
What? No good? Why? I'm dressed just the way you are. I took off all my rings. I'm not wearing make-up. I'm just a "guy."

                    ARMAND
(points to Albert's socks; they are pink)
What about those?

                    ALBERT
Oh those?... Well, one does want a hint of color. Why? What are you thinking? You're thinking that dressed this way I'm even more obvious, aren't you? You hate me. I so wanted to help you... and you both hate me. (63)

The scene is bittersweet, because the truth is there in the humor. Albert loves Val so much he's willing to pretend to be something he isn't. But he also knows it won't work and he's hurt, deeply. It is this range of emotions that transcend the merely funny to pathos. It is why Mays' work will live longer than *Dumb & Dumber* and *Ace Ventura*. While these were certainly funny, they had no real soul – no substantial or resonant theme. They existed purely for the laugh – and that's fine for the moment. But for comedy to last, it has to have a theme. May does that with *The Birdcage*.

The naked theme

And finally, sometimes you don't have to search for a theme in a story because it's stated clearly and dramatically in the most extreme fashion.

Finding the theme 63

A character can literally tell us what the story is really about, or at least give us a strong hint. In the pilot for the first season of the riveting HBO television series *True Detective* (2014–), written by Nic Pizzolatto, one of the lead detectives, Rustin Cohle, states his philosophy toward the meaning of human life, or his lack of belief in that meaning, to his partner, Martin Hart.

> COHLE
> I think that human consciousness is a tragic
> evolutionary misstep. I think that nature
> fabricated an aspect of nature that's forever
> separated from it. A creature that by natural
> law shouldn't exist.

Outside, the car passes a cheap OLD BILLBOARD with a WOMAN'S PORTRAIT on it and the legend '10/11/80: DO YOU KNOW WHO KILLED ME? CALL 800- 976-5236 REWARD' –

> COHLE
> ... I think we are things that labor under
> the illusion of having a "self," each of us
> programmed with total assurance that we're
> each a somebody. But everybody's nobody.

Cohle gets on a roll now –

> COHLE
> See, we fabricate meaning in order to
> deny what we are, so that we can keep on
> going. Family, God, country, art – these
> are the materials of our fabrications.
> We're uncanny puppets on a lonely
> planet, in cold space, living and replicating
> and sending unborn generations into
> suffering and death because that's our
> programming.

Hart's eyes have gone wide with disbelief and frustration.

> HART
> Jesus Christ.

> COHLE
> No thanks.

The deep irony of the Cohle character is that – despite his terminal fatalism – the man's determined and relentless pursuit of justice defines every episode of the entire series of *True Detective*. In a process that spans a decade, Rustin Cohle never yields in his mission to locate and punish the murderers in a brutal homicide case. The theme here is not that there's no meaning in life but that — even if there isn't — this doesn't mean life and its challenges shouldn't be experienced to their fullest possible level.

The same is sort of true in the feature film *As Good as It Gets* (1997) written by Mark Andrus and James L. Brooks. Self-centered, mean-spirited and nastily sardonic romance writer Marvin Udall has OCD and is a real bastard to his neighbors. In the opening 10 minutes, when his gay artist neighbor is looking for his pet dog, which Udall secretly just slid down the trash chute, the writers have the neighbor say directly to Udall, "You don't love anything." This becomes the underlying theme — that everyone needs love and that Udall will eventually realize that and work to achieve it. He will eventually come to love that dog, and his gay neighbor who at first he is overwhelmingly prejudiced against, and the waitress who is the only one at his favorite restaurant that can tolerate him. His journey is at first a totally selfish one. Because of his OCD he will only sit at one table and he will only allow himself to be served by that one waitress. But when she has a family issue, he helps her — not to be kind but to get her back at the restaurant so that she can serve him. The same "forced into a new journey" happens to Udall when his neighbor is robbed and becomes almost broke. Udall's status quo is disrupted and he can't work — so he reluctantly helps him to be able to go back to his norms. Udall becomes the reluctant hero and he learns the theme of the story along with the audience — that we all need love and each other.

Another film that does this is *About a Boy* (2002) written by Peter Hedges, Paul Weitz and Crag Weitz. The film opens with a game show on TV that asks the question, "Who said 'no man is an island?'" — to which the protagonist's voice-over replies "We're all islands." And thus the theme is stated and the film's conflict and hero's journey are basically announced. Will, the independently wealthy and carefree bachelor, will learn that, indeed, no man is an island. The film bookends with the final scene being set in the same room and with the same opening shot and the same TV show asking the same question — to which the protagonist's voice-over now gives a different reply.

Themes can often be stated or broadly hinted at near the very beginning of the script and the audience won't even notice, because they don't know the story yet and don't know what to look for. But when this is done, the viewer often feels a sense of completion by the end of the film; a subconscious feeling that some promise stated at the beginning has been fulfilled. And that's a nice feeling to get and to give.

What did we learn?

- Every movie and television show possesses a theme, even popular films that everyone likes. Even the comedies.
- The key to the themes that support both western and horror films is a dark force affecting peoples' lives in an isolated place outside established civilization.

The stronger the theme, the stronger the story.

Sometimes one of your characters can nakedly and obviously state your theme, or at least a version of it. They just need to be mesmerizingly eloquent when they do it.

Exercise

Examine several film or television series that you have found interesting, entertaining, or relevant to your experience. Hit all the key genres – comedy, drama, science fiction, horror, historical, western, coming of age, or romance. Write a half-page that lays out each project's theme. Now do this for the script you are writing or have written, or the script you are considering writing. If you can't find a strong theme in your own work, then you may need to adjust your approach to that work.

7 First-person narrative screenwriting

One of the most priceless moments in Charlie and Donald Kaufman's (alright, so they are really the same person, but that's the way the credits read and who the Academy Awards nominating committee named) *Adaptation* (2002) is when Charlie is sitting in a McKee screenwriting seminar, his voice-over revealing his anxiety about what he's doing there, and his craft in general, when all of a sudden McKee bellows from the stage, "And God help you if you use voice-over in your work, my friends." The voice-over suddenly stops.

For centuries books have been written in first-person narrative. We immediately identify with the storyteller, generally the protagonist – but not always. Yet, if we believe the army of books on screenwriting and the gangs of screenwriting seminars, the first-person narrative in motion pictures doesn't work and is, to quote Dickens, as dead as a doornail. Fortunately, the movie business doesn't seem to agree. For if we look at the cinema itself, theaters, the internet and DVD machines are humming with them. Just look at the recent artistic and financial successes of such movies as *About a Boy*, by Peter Hedges and Chris & Paul Weitz, *American Beauty* by Alan Ball, *Fight Club* by Jim Uhls, *The Man Who Wasn't There* by Ethan and Joel Coen, *Memento* by Christopher Nolan and *Adaptation* by Charlie and Donald Kaufman.

Narration that isn't a crutch

Without a doubt, the first-person narrator will never become a dominant style within the film business. It had been unduly shunned since the golden days of Hollywood, the 1940s thru the 1950s, when it was readily accepted as a storytelling convention in such classics as Billy Wilder's *Sunset Boulevard* and *Double Indemnity*. For a long period of time, producers, directors and even writers were persuaded to believe that using the first-person narrative was too "unrealistic", uncinematic and redundant. "Show, don't tell," became the motto. As it fell from favor and practice, the skill of writing creative first-person narrative screenplays also began to fade. Despite that, the first-person narrative has continued to grow and contribute to the art of the motion picture story, and never more than in recent years.

In 1986, Joel and Ethan Coen's *Raising Arizona* (1987) marked a significant reappearance of this otherwise dead format in screen storytelling. That same year *Stand by Me*, adapted screenplay by Raynold Gideon, and *Ferris Bueller's Day Off* by John Hughes, also dared to buck Hollywood's conventional wisdom and reposition the first-person narrator back on the big screen. While television utilized the first-person narrator in *The Wonder Years*, Hollywood believed that voice-overs in films were as passé as black and white. The industry readily accepted movies which bookended the story with narration, but seldom were the narrators heard from during the course of the film itself. The opening narration would simply be a setup for a story told in flashback. This was basically how Jean Shepard's *A Christmas Story* (written with Bob Clark and Leigh Brown) used it, with the narrator an older wiser adult looking back on an event during childhood.

The Coen brothers pushed the art of the format into a new realm in *Raising Arizona*, utilizing the first-person narrative to give us true character insight into our protagonist's view of his life and the events as they unfolded. Herein lay its creative beauty. Billy Wilder said that narration should not be used to describe what is seen, only to add to what is seen. In *Raising Arizona*, we do not hear from an older, wiser version of the main character, but from the dim-witted yet kind-hearted criminal we all learn to love and laugh at. He is no wiser, no smarter and no older by the end of the story. He is always himself, in his thoughts and deeds. Here, first-person narrative, when used creatively, makes a considerable contribution to the atmosphere, pacing and character development within the screenplay and the final film. *Raising Arizona* is a perfect example of the advancement of the art of first-person storytelling and a glimmer of the Coen masterpieces yet to come.

Hughes, however, took the first-person narrative into a new realm with his *Ferris Bueller's Day Off* (1986) by allowing the main character to turn and speak directly to the camera, breaking the fourth wall. This was not an original idea; just take a look at *Alfie*, written by Bill Naughton and based on his novel, produced in 1966, where the title character talks to the camera throughout the film. Unfortunately Hughes didn't use this lively technique throughout *Ferris Bueller's Day Off*, but the experiment did lead to some successful imitations, including television's *Malcolm in the Middle*. Once the taboo was breached, however, writers, directors and producers still did not flock to the form.

Christopher McQuarrie's Academy Award winning *The Usual Suspects* brought the first-person narrative to the forefront again in 1995. Introduced through a police interrogation this time, the narrator is a minor character, and a witness to what has transpired – a series of extended flashbacks. It wasn't until the turn of this century that the first-person narrative seems to have come into its own as a true art form.

In 1999, Ball's *American Beauty* took the Academy Awards by storm, winning Best Screenplay, Best Director and Best Picture. That same year *Fight Club* gained a tremendous following. These films began the true rebirth of creative first-person narrative in filmic storytelling. While *American Beauty* is a resurrection of *Sunset Boulevard*'s dead protagonist telling his story, the narrator, frustrated husband and business executive Lester Burnham, is a happy, smarter deceased – not a downtrodden loser. Wilder's Gillis resigns himself to his fate, as does Lester, but the latter has achieved a peace that lasts even into his death. This is the originality of Ball's work.

This takes us to the insomniac schizophrenic who is the narrator in *Fight Club* (1999). Of course, we don't know he is both of the main characters for the majority of the movie. As the narrator talks to us in voice-over and in direct-to-camera dialogue, he stops time and goes back, skips ahead or jumps around to explain a point, taking us on a ride as crazy as he is himself. Herein lies the cleverness of this disturbingly funny film, which was both acclaimed and condemned when it was released shortly after the Columbine shootings, when the conservatives wanted to protect the gun business and blamed it all on violence in the movies. One of the reasons this oddly philosophical film has generated a cult following is its creative use of first person, which originated in the novel. This is what makes the movie intoxicating; the outrageous and unexpected narration is what holds this patchwork structure of the film together.

The same can be said of the next truly creative advancement in first-person narrative, *Memento*. While Nolan doesn't use the traditional voice-over, this 2000 release is without a doubt a first-person narrative. In place of voice-over, our narrator relates his inner thoughts to an unknown entity via telephone. His commentaries, combined with his annotated Polaroids, become the narration against which the story is told in reverse order, segment by segment. Each phone call reveals more and more about our protagonist, his back-story, and his character. It becomes a fascinating ride of mental dyslexia. As in *Fight Club*, an unreliable narrator is telling the story, giving their journey its own danger and suspense while unsettling and captivating the audience at the same time.

By 2002, Peter Hedges' *About a Boy* steps forward to achieve the next advancement in the first-person narrative. What makes this underrated screenplay so unique in its use of protagonist voice-over is twofold. First, Hedges tells the story from the point of view of two main characters, both with their own voice-overs. The first-person narrative switches from character to character, scene to scene, changing our focus on the events as they transpire. Second, the narration is not offered in a past tense, as in the long history of voice-overs in movies, but in the present. The characters' inner thoughts are delivered to us as the events unfold and not as replayed commentary. The audience is mind reading the two major characters, rather than being told stories by them. Thus the audience feels immediate identification. We are truly in the characters' heads, experiencing their mistakes and understanding their motives. There is always a danger of detracting from the tension and grip of a story when one telegraphs too much, but Hedges' characters don't reveal all that much, or make redundant commentary on what we can see on the screen. Rather, they allow us to experience their personalities first hand – to get under their skin – to become them.

Charlie Kaufman follows a similar approach within his screenplay for *Adaptation* with the main character's thoughts spilling out as the action continues. The most classic moment of the film, in terms of first-person narrative, is the one mentioned earlier at the screenwriting seminar. Without being inside Kaufman's head, we will never fully feel his insecurity, which is the driving force of the character and the obstacle he must overcome to become his most successful possible self.

When it is used artistically and inventively, the first-person narrative is a viable and artistic form for the cinematic story. There is always the danger of using it as a crutch, but when used as a cane, it adds style and character.

Hard-boiled witty narration

Raymond Chandler, we believe, is the best American mystery writer of all time. It is Chandler's style and characters that everyone else emulates when creating a hard-boiled story. So Chandler was a natural pick when Billy Wilder decided to adapt James Cain's novel *Double Indemnity* for the screen. Unfortunately, Chandler was a loner who resented collaboration almost as much as he resented Hollywood. The mere fact that Chandler and Wilder ever finished a screenplay at all was a triumph. After the fact, Wilder would never work with Chandler again and soon most studios wouldn't either. But Chandler's touch in the screenplay is unmistakable. This script was included in *Best American Screenplays 3*, edited by Sam Thomas, and published by Crown in 1995. It's a perfect example of the kind of screenplay every screenwriter should read; its style, energy, and structure as fresh today as when the film produced from it was released in 1944.

Billy Wilder was a great director, but he was often close to over-dramatic and sometimes obvious as a screenwriter. *Sunset Boulevard, Some Like It Hot,* and *The Apartment* all show clear evidence of Wilder's over-the-top view of dramatics. Chandler's novels are the opposite. His writing is clever, sarcastic and subtle, which may have been one of the major reasons the two didn't get along. It's quite interesting that Wilder never fired Chandler, only complained about him. Obviously, Wilder recognized Chandler's skill as a writer – it was his personality he couldn't stand.

All of Chandler's hard-boiled books are written in first-person narrative, so it was a natural fit to have Chandler work on Cain's hard-boiled first-person narrative *Double Indemnity* (1944), which focuses on an insurance agent seduced into helping a woman kill her husband for the insurance. For a taste of the film's bitter tone, just take a look at this speech . . .

> WALTER (V.O.)
> It was mid-afternoon, and it was funny, I can still
> remember the smell of honeysuckle all along the block.
> I felt like a million. There was no way in the world
> I could have known that murder can sometimes
> smell like honeysuckle.

Here's the hook, less than 5 minutes into it. It falls at the same time in the film and in the same manner as in *American Beauty* and *Sunset Boulevard*. Chandler and Wilder were both masters at the hook. But we believe that it was Chandler who kept the hard-boiled wit working throughout the voice-over narrations of the screenplay.

> WALTER (V.O.)
> Only what I didn't know then was that I wasn't
> playing her. She was playing me – with a marked deck
> – and the stakes weren't any blue and yellow chips.
> They were dynamite.

This little insight from our protagonist gives the whole shooting match away – except no one realizes it at the time. By the end of the film we discover that Phyllis had murdered her husband's first wife and is only using Neff to kill her husband. But the wittiness of the lines disguises the fact that the writers have just told us the twist ending. The droll cockiness of the main character comes over through the narration, and seldom through the actual dialogue. The narration is written more in Chandler's style, or from the book, while the sometimes over-dramatic dialogue is Wilder's. The contrast is one of the things that make this screenplay and film so fascinating. It's like two different people: the inner Neff – ironic, sarcastic and aware of his faults – and the outer Neff – trying too hard, giving in to emotional forces of lust and pride so much as not to realize when he's not being smart. Oddly enough, this works extremely well. Without the narration, we wouldn't care about Neff or understand his addiction to the intrigue that sets his ultimate destruction in motion.

The character of Keyes, in the insurance investigator friend of Neff, has the best dialogue. And it's his words that resonate under Neff's voice-over narration.

> KEYES
> They've committed a murder and that's not like
> taking a trolley ride together where each one can
> get off at a different stop. They're stuck with each
> other. They've got to ride all the way to the end
> of the line. And it's a one-way trip, and the
> last stop is the cemetery.

The trolley simile works throughout the screenplay, as when Phyllis says, "It's straight down the line for both us, remember." The "straight down the line" phrase having been used in act I and act II of the film finally comes into clear focus in act III when Keyes gives us the full trolley ride simile. It becomes the theme – once you start on a ride you have to see it through to the end of the line; there's just no jumping off. It's doubtful the connection between the trolley line similes and the death by falling off a train was accidental.

How does it speak to you as a writer? In *Double Indemnity*, it is the power of the narration that captures the audience and carries the story. The wit, the moral dilemmas, the intelligence of the character: these are only revealed through the narration. This is first-person narration at its classic best.

Found footage as first person

During Hollywood's Golden Age, the 1947 production *Lady in the Lake*, screenplay by Steve Fisher, based on the novel by Raymond Chandler, endeavored to create a much more personal first-person narrative beyond the simple use of a voice-over. The entire movie was shot from the point of view of its classic hard-boiled lead character, Philip Marlowe, who, as he investigates the usual film noir case of murder, avarice and treachery, is unseen by the audience except for when he looks in a mirror, window or some other reflective surface. Needless to say, all of Marlowe's dialogue was presented through voice-over. In this film, the subjective camera approach was a stylistic choice as opposed to an attempt at creating an experience supposedly recorded in real time in a genuine, true-to-life setting. The experiment was deemed a failure and not repeated, at least in the case of an entire film noir being shot via a subjective camera.

However, starting with *Cannibal Holocaust* (written by Gianfranco Clerici) in 1980, the illusion of a singular point of view through a subjective camera was developed via a mock-documentary found-footage style that gave the audience the false impression that a first-person narrative is being actively created in real time. "Found footage" literally means the images the viewer is witnessing are actual documentary film or video that has been purportedly recovered and edited for their entertainment. In this sub-genre, a movie is not some fictional creation but a recording as authentic as the nightly news.

From *Cannibal Holocaust*, then *The Last Broadcast* and *The Blair Witch Project* in 1998 and 1999 respectively, and moving on to a new wave of films like *Paranormal Activity*, *Cloverfield*, and *VHS*, the found-footage project or approach has redefined the first-person narrative. The limitations of this style of production can match its advantages. In a film with a first-person voice-over, the protagonist may roam the entire world of a story, or at least that part of it the protagonist can physically visit, with scenes being covered from different angles like any classically produced movie. But in found-footage films the singular point of view is usually restricted to what the protagonist(s) can record via handheld devices, cameras, or phones. While this approach may limit a writer's options in exploring their story's universe, it does create a sense of verisimilitude that can be quite forceful or striking, literally grabbing an audience's attention by their eyeballs. This is particularly effective in genre films like suspense thrillers, science-fiction projects, and horror movies. It can also be an advantage to budget and production with the ragged or unfinished image of the supposedly recovered footage relatively simple to produce while still effectively supporting the creative conceit.

An excellent example of a successful found-footage project is *Chronicle* (2012) with a screenplay by Max Landis and a story by Landis and Josh Trank. Like many of today's films, *Chronicle* is a mixture of genres – in this case, science fiction, thriller, and coming of age. When a teenager, Andrew Detmer and some of his friends stumble on an alien artifact in a cave, they all gain superpowers that dramatically change their lives. In Andrew's case, this is disastrous since, as the opening scene establishes, his drunken father has severely damaged his psyche and emotional development. The found-footage approach is particularly effective here in establishing the point of view of a distressed character ...

```
FROM ANDREW'S FIRST CAMERA.

CUT – to indicate time lapses within a scene.

INT. DETMER RESIDENCE – ANDREW'S ROOM

The room is dingy. Unkempt. The camera sits on the bed, on its side,
facing the door. We can hear someone moving around off-screen.

The door handle clicks; someone's trying it. Then nothing.
Then, suddenly, loud pounding on the door.

Andrew's voice is scratchy and prone to cracking. He speaks
with a rushed mix of fear and anxiety.

                    ANDREW (O.S.)
    What do you want, I'm getting ready for school-

                    MR. DETMER (O.S.)
    Why is the door locked, unlock this fucking door right now.

The bed stirs as Andrew sits down.

                    MR. DETMER (O.S.) (CONT'D)
    I said unlock this door. UNLOCK THE DOOR. OPEN THE DOOR, NOW.

                    ANDREW (O.S.)
    You're drunk –

                    MR. DETMER (O.S.)
    Listen, you don't tell me – IF I'M DRUNK, OR...
```

```
                    ANDREW (O.S.)
It's seven thirty. In the AM. You're drunk, dad, that's
crazy –

                  MR. DETMER (O.S.)
What're you doing in there?

                    ANDREW (O.S.)
I'm filming this.

                  MR. DETMER (O.S.)
What?

                    ANDREW (O.S.)
I bought a camera. I'm filming all your shit from now on.
```

There's a beat, and then we can hear Mr. Detmer moving away from the door.

Note the distinct formatting that defines the script as a found-footage production. The initial setting and action lines – FROM ANDREW'S FIRST CAMERA, *CUT – to indicate time lapses within a scene* – establish the subjective camera technique that will record the entire story. The cutting into a scene, giving the audience the impression that the found footage has been edited for time, is actually defined within the script by the writer. When Andrew speaks, since he is behind the camera, his lines are all denoted as O.S. or off-screen. It must be noted that, in the final film, Andrew is visible in this scene thanks to a mirror on his bedroom's door that reveals him operating his camera on a tripod erected by his bed. This was a smart directorial choice that enhanced the moment – especially when an angry Mr. Detmer banged on the door, making the mirror and Andrew's image shake. The scene also quickly established the world of the story, its hero's predicament, and his need for a camera, all within less than two strong pages.

Throughout a found-footage screenplay, some type of this format should be followed to maintain the illusion of a real-time recorded and edited experience. There have been films, like *End of Watch*, that cheat on this technique, mixing scenes shot with ordinary omniscient cinematography with those using the found-footage method. While this was extremely successful in the case of *End of Watch*, the film's writer/director, David Ayer, was an established talent at the time he produced the project. For a novice writing a spec found-footage screenplay, it's probably best to stick to a consistent approach, at least on paper.

Mockumentary

The mockumentary has invaded television, being employed in almost every style or genre of series, including science-fiction dramas like *The River* and premium HBO comedies like *The Comeback*. One of the most successful was

The Office (2005–2013), a half-hour network series in which each episode is supposedly part of a massive documentary covering the work lives of a cadre of corporate drones trapped in the office of the fictional Dunder Mifflin paper company. Within the conceit of the production of the documentary, in-between cinéma-vérité style moments where we witness the company's employees interact, we are offered talking head interviews and even occasional glimpses of the documentary crew. The dialogue scenes are written in standard script format interspersed with the isolated interviews.

In the episode "E-Mail Surveillance", written by Jennifer Celotta, the manager of the office, Michael Scott, experiences abject rejection and humiliation, as the character inevitably did in almost every episode. His first interview in the script defines its premise …

MICHAEL TALKING HEAD

                    MICHAEL
There are some things a boss can't share with his employees.
His salary - that would just depress them. His bed. (gets lost
in thought, then) I also can't tell them I'm going to be reading
their e-mails. E-mail surveillance. All the big companies do it.
Increases efficiency. Increases productivity. It is a necessary
evil. Well, not really evil. It is a necessary good thing.

The series' dialogue is that most difficult of literary creations – natural-appearing ersatz conversation that is anything but ordinary talk. This is an illusion of normal, human conversation woven into scenes that tend to be short and extremely concise, which helps create the realistic and immediate atmosphere a project like this requires.

INT. OFFICE - JIM AND DWIGHT'S DESKS

Michael comes out of his office. His tie is off and a few buttons
on his shirt are unbuttoned. He wanders over to Jim's desk.

                    MICHAEL (a little down)
Hey.

                    JIM
Hi.

                    DWIGHT
Where's your tie?

                    MICHAEL
I don't know. I just wanted to take it off. Sometimes work
can be so damn frustrating. You know what I mean Jim?

                    JIM
Uh, yeah, I guess.

                    DWIGHT
What's wrong, Michael? Talk to me.

                    MICHAEL
It's just the same old crap. The boss is riding my ass.

                    DWIGHT (alarmed)
Oh, God. Jan? What's going on?

                    MICHAEL
I don't know. I don't want to talk about it. I just want to
hang out here where I'm just one of the guys.

                    DWIGHT
The most important one of the guys.

                    MICHAEL
That's not the point.

Jim looks to camera – point? What's the point?

                    DWIGHT (quietly, but intense)
It's exactly the point. You've hit a slump. Happens to the
best. But you have to remember who you are. How've hard you've
worked for this. You are the boss. You can buy and sell
all of us with a snap of your little finger.

                    MICHAEL
I'd never do that.

                    JIM (to Dwight)
And you can't actually snap with your little finger.

                    DWIGHT (to Jim)
This hardly seems the time.

                    MICHAEL
No, this is great. This is perfect. Just us, out here, doing
some friendly ribbing. The group of us. The worker bees.

Jim looks to the camera. What the hell?

To push *The Office's* subjective approach further during production, the scripts would be shot and covered as written, then the actors were allowed or encouraged to improvise. This could produce a tremendous amount of footage, usually too much for a half-hour show, which would lead to challenging sessions in the editing room. This was not a serious problem in the case of *The Office* with its informal documentary style, gifted cast, and talented production crew. However, a warning must be offered to productions that aren't so blessed in these respective areas. Improvised material may be difficult if not impossible to effectively edit thanks to uneven performance and production. Within the found-footage approach, improvisation may appear appealing but, without the proper cast or resources, a refined-looking product might be elusive.

In the case of another found-footage television project, *Modern Family* (2009–), the concept of a documentary crew following an ordinary American family is loosely instituted. As in *The Office*, there are talking head sequences, but the documentary crew is never seen or referred to. Outside of the interviews, the characters in *Modern Family* interact like any characters in any TV show, including within highly personal and intimate moments at work, in bed, or in the bathroom; places or situations no documentary crew would probably ever witness. The mockumentary *cinéma-vérité* style appears to be a stylistic device used to comment on the action as opposed to a true found-footage approach. An example can be seen in the scene below from the series pilot, which was written by Steven Levitan and Christopher Lloyd.

```
INTERVIEW - PHIL

                    PHIL
     I'm the cool dad. That's my thing. I'm hip. I surf the web,
     I have an iPhone, I know a lot of the dances from "High School
     Musical."

INT. PHIL & CLAIRE'S HOUSE - PAST

Phil demonstrates a dance from "High School Musical" as his hor-
rified kids look on.

                    PHIL
                 (singing)
     WE'RE ALL IN THIS TOGETHER, YES WE ARE ...
```

This series' dialogue scenes also tend to be longer and more formal in their structure and intent than in *The Office*, although it's rare for a scene to exceed two pages. In this case, *Modern Family* employs a "fake" found-footage style to give its scenes a fresh, natural feel. Considering the show has won multiple Emmys through several seasons, any criticism that this method is inauthentic to the found-footage technique might be considered moot.

In any case, *Chronicle*, *The Office*, and *Modern Family* clearly establish that a first-person narrative approach should not necessarily be limited to a protagonist's voice-over commenting on the action. The development and refinement of this technique is clearly still in flux and, depending on the project and its intentions, a first persona narration, found footage or faux documentary style may offer a screenwriter some interesting creative opportunities.

What did we learn?

Use first-person narration carefully or it can be a story crutch.
Hard-boiled narration can be a cliché or a strong element in a solid story.
First-person narrative has evolved from the original, hard-boiled detective voice-over used in film noir into a variety of challenging new approaches.
Found footage is the new first-person narration, especially in mockumentaries.

Exercise

For this exercise you will write four scenes. The first will be a found-footage scene set in a time and place you're familiar with. The second will be a found-footage scene set in a time and place you're not familiar with. Now take these two scenes and turn each of them into voice-over narration with no found-footage aspect.

If you are currently writing a screenplay, write a found-footage scene – supposedly shot with a phone or camcorder at a birthday party, workplace event, wedding, etc. – that could potentially fit into that project. You may be surprised at how useful such a scene could be.

8 Managing multiple-protagonist syndrome or ensembles

Most stories are told through a central protagonist. Whether this is in books, short stories, plays or screenplays, the story has a main character that is faced with a goal and obstacles and eventually makes some kind of change. But what happens when we have more than one such character in our story? How do we navigate their multiple journeys without losing sight of them all or slighting any one of them?

Ensemble vs. episodic

First, let's differentiate what is an ensemble story from what is an ensemble cast or an episodic story. The ensemble cast is a group that goes off on the same journey together – as in many horror films and war movies. The group becomes the main character, with the leader our main protagonist. Non-genre examples of ensemble casts include Frank Darabont's *The Green Mile* and Elaine May's *The Birdcage*. Here there is a small cast of central characters that last throughout the film, becoming our family and the family of the story who take us on their mutual adventure.

An episodic screenplay will contain several complete stories all linked in some way. *Pulp Fiction* links its separate short stories via common characters that cross over from one tale to the next. McKellar & Girard's *The Red Violin* artistically links the stories of several people who come into the possession of the titled object. The separate stories are complete in themselves, like short stories in a printed collection. While they may provide backstory for each other, they can each stand alone.

The ensemble screenplay is one that has multiple stories progressing independently but simultaneously, each linked to the others in some manner, the very least of which being by time and place. Often these separate stories strike against each other at some given time, usually crossing, intersecting or colliding with one another. They are interwoven into a unique fabric that, without each strand, would unravel and fall apart. But besides linking our multiple protagonists by time and place, these separate stories are often linked by something else, such as a shared theme or goal.

The classic example of the ensemble screenplay is *American Graffiti* (1973). Screenwriters George Lucas, Gloria Katz, and Willard Huyck wrote an engaging story of a group of high school graduates on the last day of summer in Modesto, California in 1962. Linked by their friendship and this time and place, each character is set off on their own journey of discovery as to who they really are. Each has a pretense, a mask that they put up to hide behind and for the outside world to see; one they will each drop by the end of the night, coming to a better understanding of who they are and what they might really want. They meet at their usual hang-out, Mel's drive-in, only to separate and eventually reunite by the end, each having experienced a change and gaining a new outlook on life. Here the four main protagonists are linked not only by friendship, time and place, but by the theme of their individual stories.

Andy Breckman uses a common goal for his comedy *Rat Race* (2001). The separate characters, all strangers, suddenly find themselves competing to find a million dollars in hidden money. They separate and face their own hilarious obstacles along the journey to riches, only to meet up again and defeat their common foe, the millionaire that started the race as a form of degrading entertainment. Thus, Breckman changes the characters' underlying commonality from greed to revenge – or at least getting even.

In *Love Actually* (2003), writer director Richard Curtis connects his protagonists by relationship first. The Prime Minister likes the woman living next door to the secretary of his sister's husband, who works with a woman who won't commit to a relationship with a fellow workmate. Other links abound as these various stories of romance and lost love criss-cross and pass one another. One of the faults of this film is that some of the stories are not well tied into the fold or tied up by the end of the picture. But again, the underlying theme that binds all these characters together is the intersection of love and lust, asking the question, "Which is stronger?" The goal of all the characters is the same, to find love.

Linking stories

What are some tricks of the trade and coping mechanisms for dealing with multiple protagonist syndrome? First, it is generally a good idea to carefully plan out exactly how you are going to link each of your character's stories and what each character's goal, obstacle and outcome will be. During the writing process you will no doubt find new and fun ways to have these stories intersect and by-pass each other. How they collide and separate, only to collide again, is what makes an ensemble work. Are they related? Do they work in the same place? Do they cross each other's paths often?

We never know which character or characters we'll collide with again and again, yet this randomness seems to occur more often than would seem logical. Are we all connected somehow within the universe? Is Einstein right re: his theory of unity and is randomness a part of this unity? Perhaps these are universal deep thoughts within our psyche and the reason why many of us find ensemble stories so interesting? Hey, if you don't like one character, wait a few minutes and maybe you'll prefer the next one.

Playing with time

Another way to link the stories in an ensemble drama is to play with time and place while still somehow interconnecting the characters. This can involve moving from one location or period of time to another for dramatic effect, thereby not following any linear approach at all. Considering that a writer is already attempting to manage multiple characters and their worlds in an ensemble piece, layering in a timeline that's out of chronological order can be extremely challenging. But when writers pull it off, like Quentin Tarantino and Roger Avary did in their screenplay for *Pulp Fiction*, the results can produce a classic that arguably set a template for this time-shattering approach.

As diverse a slate of films as *Babel, Dunkirk, Inception, The Grudge, The Dark Knight Rises*, and *Eternal Sunshine of the Spotless Mind* have contained nonlinear structures. In all of these pieces, there is some kind of linking device that ties the stories and their characters together. In *Dunkirk*, it was the men trapped on the beach, surrounded by Nazi troops, and the men trying to save them. In *Eternal Sunshine of the Spotless Mind*, it was memory and what it truly means to the human condition. And in *Babel*, it's as simple as a single 0.270 caliber Winchester 60 rifle.

A look at *Babel* (2006), written by Guillermo Arriaga, will give us an idea of how this approach can work. The film begins with two Arab shepherd teenagers in Morocco as they take the Remington rifle their father has given them into the hills to shoot the jackals hounding their small herd of goats. However, as the two young boys play around with this lethal weapon, they accidentally shoot an American woman riding by in a tourist bus. This launches a series of events that not only severely affect the lives of the boys and their families but keys us into three other stories – the woman and her husband on the bus, their children and their Mexican nanny in Los Angeles, and a deaf Japanese girl in Tokyo. As the film progresses, the story, which moves back and forth in time, has a domino effect not unlike the Ben Franklin poem about the nail and the horse, which goes:

> For the want of a nail the shoe was lost,
> For the want of a horse the rider was lost,
> For the want of a rider the battle was lost
> For the want of a battle the kingdom was lost
> And all for the want of a horseshoe-nail.

In this case, because the American woman is shot, her husband calls their kids' nanny to inform her she can't go to her son's wedding in Mexico because they'll be delayed returning home. Which leads the nanny into taking the two young children to Mexico with her, which leads to dire consequences for all three of them. And also leads the authorities to track down the Japanese girl's father because he originally owned the weapon, which his wife used to kill herself, which, in turn, had dire emotional significance for his daughter. While the children and their parents are obviously linked personally, the only element that truly connects all of these people who are located in four different countries is the rifle. We learn at the end of the film that the Japanese girl's father originally owned the Remington but gave it to a hunting guide he had hired in Morocco, who in turn sold it to the shepherd boy's father. If it weren't for the rifle, the initial, tragic incident of the suicide of the Japanese girl's mother and all the events of the film that basically follow from it would never have occurred. This serves the film's central theme of how all the people of this world are interconnected in some fashion – the so-called butterfly effect – and how one violent act – one woman's suicide – can create a terrible sequence of events that can affect many lives. To paraphrase Ben Franklin, for want of a single life so many were lost.

Ensemble characters

Which brings us to character. While it is always important to make each and every character in your story a distinct and engrossing individual, it is even more important in the ensemble. The audience must be able to recognize who is who quickly and succinctly. Your characters may begin as stereotypes to give the audience an easy handle to latch onto, but they must quickly move out of the stereotype into uniqueness. The viewer must be able to recognize whose story they have switched to instantly so as not to be confused and miss essential plot information. This can be accomplished a number of ways, two of them being with location and speech pattern.

David Mamet uses the dialogue style in his wonderful ensemble screenplay, *State and Main* (2000), to help the viewer instantly recognize who is associated with which story. All the movie company characters talk in a fast staccato and rarely even finish a sentence, speaking in fragments, trailing off, switching subjects in mid-conversation and constantly interrupting each other. We, the viewers, know instantly whose story we are in: the world of a bunch of Hollywood wackos, when the pace of the dialogue becomes so frantic. Once the dialogue changes to a slow, drawn-out pace with complete, yet often meaningless sentences, we instantly know that we are in the world of the townies and the story of the bookstore owner.

The screenwriter character is the one that transverses these two tales. His dialogue matches that of the townies, yet he is one of the film people. His goal is to learn what he truly wants. The bookstore owner's goal is to get out of a relationship of convenience and find someone who shares her love of literature and life. The film director's goal is to finish his film before the star can get arrested again. Their three stories are linked by time and place, but also by the screenwriter character himself.

Recurring locations

The recurring use of location can be another simple way to help the audience keep track of all the colliding stories and multiple characters. In *Big Trouble* (2002), adapted for the screen by Robert Ramsey and Matthew Stone from Dave Barry's novel, the screenplay manages to juggle a number of characters and action scenes without losing track of each person's dilemma. As in most ensemble pieces, the characters are introduced fairly quickly, each displayed in their status quo. There is the Herk family – mother Anna, teenage daughter Jenny and total jerk stepfather Arthur – all of them introduced watching TV in their expensive Florida home – along with their pretty Hispanic maid Nina.

Into this location, specifically the backyard, enters Puggy the vagrant, the teenagers Matt and Andrew who want to shoot Jenny with a water pistol for a school game, and two hitmen from New Jersey, Leonard and Henry, who have been hired to kill Arthur. Next to join this bizarre collection of people is Elliot (Matt's divorced father) and the cops Monica and Walter, who arrive as a result of Matt being mistaken for a killer when he dashes into the house to squirt Jenny. Thus, virtually all the characters collide in this single location and they do so very early on in the story. This allows us to quickly visualize who is who and how they relate in this soon to be convoluted story. The TV room will become a recurring location and the shooting of the TV a recurring action that marks the progression of the story.

Another recurring collision location is the bar run by the Russian arms smugglers. It is into this location that Puggy first arrives along with two stupid ex-cons, Eddie and Snake, who will eventually find their way into the Herk's TV room with everyone else. It is here that Arthur buys a bomb and meets the two ex-cons and it is here that the two FBI agents are first introduced near the end of the story.

This revisitation of location and action helps pull together the disjointed nature of *Big Trouble*'s ensemble story. What Barry and the screenwriters do well is to interweave the characters, allowing them to collide once and then again as if being given a second chance, but with more complications piled onto the situation. By bringing back these locations and actions, the audience is given a chance to catch their breath and recognize all the characters and what they have experienced so far. Thus the story virtually has its own catch-up time by bringing us back to safe and familiar surroundings. While recurring actions may be predictable, especially in a comedy, they also become reassuring in an otherwise confusing atmosphere.

Big Trouble has a large ensemble to keep track of, with 11 central characters – not counting the dog Roger and his arch nemesis toad, the two Russian weapon dealers, or the two FBI agents. Yet we never lose sight of any of the characters or their goals thanks to the use of recurring locations and actions, places and activities where these absurd people all continue to collect and thus can be easily sorted out by the audience.

The ensemble anchor

Another trick is to select one of the many personalities of the ensemble to be the anchor in the sea of stories. By letting one character's story have more weight, the audience is given a safe place to return to – a home to rest in before venturing out into the world of the story again. The Coen brothers do this extremely well in their film *Fargo* (1996). Even though Margie, the policewoman, isn't introduced until almost 20 minutes into the film, she becomes the anchor for the entire film. A triple homicide in the opening scene is the incident which connects three plot lines – a small town police woman, Margie, trying to solve the murders; Jerry, a dishonest car dealer trying to get out of a legal jam by extorting money from his mean father-in-law by staging the kidnapping of his wife; and the story of Carl, one of the kidnappers, who wants to get away from his aggravating and dangerous partner in crime who perpetrated the triple homicide after the kidnapping.

Even though the film begins with Jerry and the kidnappers, and then follows the kidnappers first – going back to Jerry at the car dealership and his pressures from his insurance swindle gone wrong – the last introduced character, Margie, is the only person who experiences a true character arc. She becomes our anchor and the only one to live happily ever after. The Coen brothers switch back and forth between their three protagonists often enough for us to never lose track of them, yet staying with each story long enough to keep us invested in their tales.

John Cleese introduces all his main characters in quick clean strokes in his screenplay for the film *A Fish Called Wanda* (1988), like a fisherman throwing out the line over and over. These glimpses give us a capsulated insight into each character, a handle on what to expect from them.

Cleese quickly establishes the premise of the story, a jewelry heist, but uses the meeting of the gang to also set up many things to come – herein lies Cleese's skill. He wastes no time in setting up the conflict between the animal lover Ken and the somewhat out-of-it killer Otto, who views all creatures as insects – this antagonistic relationship will lead to a showdown later.

Similarly he subtly sets up the subtext of Ken's hidden love for Wanda, the girlfriend of his boss, the gangster George, by having him call his fish Wanda. He also establishes that this story will be full of double-crosses right away with Wanda passing off Otto as her brother, when he's obviously her lover.

But the main character that has an arc is the barrister Archie, and although he is shown in court for a glimpse during the credits and then a fast look at his boring home life where he is ignored and taken for granted by both wife and daughter early on (maybe a total of 1 minute in scenes), once the heist gets started he is left out of the film for some time. When he resurfaces as the boss's defense attorney, we remember him like an old friend and suddenly we realize that he will, indeed, play an important part in the film. As Archie becomes George's defense attorney, he replaces George in the story. He becomes the person Wanda seduces and Otto is jealous of. But also, he begins to have the majority of scenes while George is left behind, hardly appearing at all. Thus Cleese changes the focus of his ensemble story from George and the diamonds to Archie and his need to be reinvigorated with life. George's adventure changes his life as well as Wanda's.

The challenge in any ensemble is how many of the characters will make a change. It must not be forced upon everyone, but to those on whom it seems appropriate. These changes must be set up from the beginning, then nudged along as Cleese does so well in *Wanda*. Yes, it is a farce and somewhat standard in form, but the fly fishing is what keeps it exciting – the glimpses back and forth from character to character that all connect.

The fun of writing the ensemble screenplay is seeing how madly we can shuffle the deck but still end the trick with the cards somehow back in some kind of order. It's what we all want to believe about life – that order is at the root of all chaos, that things happen for a reason, that we can all learn and change. The danger in writing the ensemble screenplay is dropping the deck and losing some cards. As any magician will tell you, keep those cards moving, not so fast that the audience gets confused and gives up watching, but just fast enough to keep them a little unsure while intrigued. Then the ending will pay off big.

Ensemble in the park

In 2002 the movie *Gosford Park* was nominated for seven Academy Awards and brought home the Oscar for Best Original Screenplay. Screenwriter Julian Fellowes would go on to even more acclaim, especially in television where he created and wrote the internationally popular *Downton Abbey*. By looking at his work on *Gosford Park* we can see how he established his own approach to tackling the complexities of ensemble storytelling by virtually ignoring story. In *Gosford Park*, Fellowes presents a weekend outing of an aging aristocratic family and its friends at the end of the era of grand houses and proud servants. More than he did in *Downton Abbey* with its dual stories of upper class and servant class, Fellowes combines the servants of the guests with the guest themselves. Into this mix he charts many distinct courses with a large assemblage of characters.

With 14 upper class, 14 servants, and two working class policemen, there are a lot of people to keep track of. What Fellowes does is utilize the "outsider" as a prime factor in the storytelling and in keeping track of his extended cast. Upstairs, Fellowes has the aristocracies mix with some less-than-proper types, among them a performer and a film producer from Hollywood. It is against these characters as a backdrop that we can better distinguish the goings on of the other characters. How each one of the upper-crust family relates to these outsiders becomes a way for the viewer to keep track of each mini story.

Downstairs, Fellowes does the same with the servants, who have their own class system. Here we meet the new maid to the matriarch, Mary, through whose eyes we see the world of the serving class, as well as Henry, the valet to the movie producer. While Mary is at home with her role in society, she is new to the place and the people who run the household. Conversely, Fellowes gives us her opposite in Henry, a manservant who seems out of place and ignorant of his station.

Fellowes thus offers the audience several characters to identify with. The stiff nose-in-the-air upper crust of England is not a society that most moviegoers have experience with or could empathize with. Nor can most viewers feel a connection with lifelong professional servants. The era of these stations has long since passed and never truly existed in countries such as the United States or Canada. To get the audience into the characters, Fellowes presents us with some tour guides – the outsiders. As they learn the ropes downstairs and feel the pettiness upstairs, so does the viewer.

But Fellowes doesn't just use the outsiders of *Gosford Park* as guides; they are also the sign of what's to come. They are the future, a time that we, the viewers, already inhabit. While the old-guard characters are determined to stay the course, their very existence is becoming retired. The wealthy gentry are losing their wealth while the working class business couple is the only one that remains happy, both financially and domestically. By the same token, the only guests having any fun seem to be the outsiders – the performer cousin who is here just for kicks and the movie producer here for research – but always on the phone to Hollywood (a foreshadowing of the cell-phone-dealing Hollywood yet to come).

The two policemen reflect this same approach to character. Fellowes gives us the standard old-school Scotland Yard inspector, who enjoys talking with the gentry and touching the evidence. He is totally incompetent and incapable of solving anything. Yet his new constable assistant is mindful of the need not to move anything or contaminate evidence. The new policeman knows the right questions to ask, but is prevented from doing so by the old way of doing things. Thus, the case goes unclosed and no arrest is made.

Fellowes' use of the outsider surviving and going on while the old guard begins to crumble is the underlying theme of *Gosford Park*. The ensemble approach works exceptionally well here. While many of the old gentry seem to merge in our minds, this may have even been Fellowes' purpose. They are all alike, dying antiques of a by-gone day. It is the new fresh outsiders that stand out as memorable and it is they who shall inherit the future.

The trouble with ensemble

Alfred Hitchcock may have been a great director of suspense, but when it came to comedy, even black comedy, he barely ranked. This is obvious from *The Trouble with Harry* (1955), screenplay by Michael Hayes based on the novel by Jack Trevor Story. Hayes worked hard to transfer the charm of Story's story about a corpse found in the woods that several people think they may have killed and several others help in hiding the body, only to discover that he died of a heart attack. Harry is buried and dug up six times for various reasons and Hayes added many humorous lines within the screenplay that were all but killed deader than Harry himself by the lethargic pace.

Early on, the painter Mr. Marlow interrupts the Captain as he is about to drag the body away, erroneously believing that he shot the man while rabbit hunting.

                    MARLOW
Does he live around here?

                    CAPTAIN
Well, he died around here, that's what counts.

The potential of this clever dialogue is lost, not due to the actor's delivery, but to the incredibly lugubrious pace of the scene as its lines are spoken, transporting most viewers into their own daydreams. Several other charming moments and clever script ideas are equally belittled, such as when the deputy sheriff shows the artist the pastel sketch of the corpse, asking where he saw the model. Mr. Marlow claims it was a muse from within, which he demonstrates by taking the sketch and redrawing, altering the incriminating evidence.

Why didn't this ensemble dark comedy work? First, because Hitchcock made too much of a conscious effort to make the movie "cute." The stakes are way too low and the humor too malnourished in this film. Serene shots of autumn woods and cute music litter the film like tossed away milk duds, melting as a gooey mess into the narrative. The script lacks tension and suspense. The dialogue is too light-hearted and the characters express such little apprehension over the dead Harry or who killed him; the audience never invests in the plot or the characters themselves. Nothing seems important or dire, even though the characters continue to say that things are. They just say it with such nonchalance that it doesn't seem to matter.

The potential risks of an ensemble dark comedy are fully illustrated in *The Trouble with Harry*. While we watch four different main characters whose lives become intertwined as a result of the discovery and disposal of the body, none of them are well developed. Each is given a light dusting, an off-handed simplicity that's geared toward the simplicity of the film itself. For example, when the millionaire character wants to buy Marlow's paintings, he refuses money and only asks for simple little items for each of his newfound friends and co-conspirators. He also proposes to a woman he's known for all of one day (a woman who hated her husband because he was "too good" as she put it).

The script does move between the characters well, but each of the scenes lacks any conflict, they simply add more exposition. Perhaps it was the time period that the script and movie were developed in. Some might argue that today's audiences are too impatient and need faster-paced stories. But the trouble here is a lack of convincing character development and narrative urgency.

For an ensemble story to work, each of the characters must grip and entice the audience, making them want to find out what will happen to them. The trouble with *The Trouble with Harry* is that it didn't.

Ensemble in television

Dating back to the soap operas which used to infest North American daytime hours, or the telenovelas that are still broadcast everywhere in Latin America, multiple character concepts have been and will continue to be rife in television. Whether it's the arcane and bizarre, like *Lost* or *The Walking Dead*, the work-centric comedic and interconnected domestic, like *The Office* or *Modern Family*, or Wall Street shenanigans and multi-generational drama, like *Billions* or *This Is Us*, there are many potential approaches to explore ensemble character structures in this medium.

The added advantage of this format is that multiple story lines and extended populations can provide escalating narrative energy for a series that will sustain many seasons. An added benefit is that, since there are often several lead characters, the loss or departure of an actor or two is not usually fatal to the endurance of the show. *Law & Order* not only survived numerous cast changes throughout its 20 seasons and 456 episodes, it fostered several successful spin-offs.

However, while there are distinct advantages to the ensemble television drama, there are unique challenges as well. It's difficult to develop two or three appealing and sustainable characters for a television project, let alone many more, and the production and structural issues posed by myriad locations and storylines can be daunting.

Dan Fogelman's pilot script for *This Is Us* (2016–), which was originally entitled *36* in reference to the shared birth dates of four of its main characters, is an almost picture-perfect representative of what an ensemble project should look like when the right creative choices have been made. The series' central theme – how the decisions we make as individuals can resonate and reverberate throughout the generations that follow us – is strong enough to nourish several seasons of fresh, ever-evolving and engrossing drama. The characters – well defined and distinct from each other, yet still flawed and human – are not only identifiable and accessible but also imminently castable. The world – 1970s Pittsburgh intercut with contemporary New Jersey and Los Angeles – is visually appealing yet still producible on a television budget. And finally there is an extra element that is so often absent from ensemble drama – a touch of humor to liven the proceedings and create a distinct sense of character appeal.

A close look at the pilot script will not only illustrate the manner in which time and location can be used to create tension and interest but also how the creative choices made between the first or primary production draft and the final aired episode can not only produce a better show but properly launch an entire series.

Let us begin with the *This is Us* flashback structure. In most ensemble dramas – such as *Lost*, *Mad Men*, or *The Walking Dead* – the manner in which the flashbacks are employed is clearly defined and unambiguous. A character experiences a moment in present time, then we directly cut to an incident in the past that comments on or dramatically enhances or enriches the present in some way.

In the pilot for *This is Us*, the story is structured around three sets of characters in two widely separated timelines and three distinct locations – Jack and Rebecca, a married couple expecting triplets in late 1970s Pittsburgh; Kate and Kevin, a brother and sister struggling to overcome career and relationship obstacles respectively in contemporary Los Angeles; and Randall, a successful executive and family man living in modern New York, who is seeking out the biological father he's never known. Thanks to the careful treatment of the 1970s Pittsburgh scenes in the pilot – we never see cars, appliances, clothing, or other cultural artifacts that clearly define the era until the episode's climax – the audience initially has no idea that Jack and Rebecca are not sharing the same timeline as the other characters.

Making Randall, his family, and his long-lost father all African American also immediately dissuades us from thinking that any of them have any relationship with the very white Kevin and Kate or Jack and Rebecca. When we reach the climax of the episode and realize Jack and Rebecca adopted Randall as a baby; that he has been raised as a brother to Kate and Kevin as part of the "Big Three", and that all of these characters are directly and personally related, it comes as a totally unexpected but satisfying shock. This sly use of flashbacks not only produced an entertaining and surprising pilot, it was a superlative way to launch the series. We learned enough about all the characters' backgrounds, subjective issues, and challenges to become engaged with their distinct story lines on a basic, dramatic level.

But, again, it's not only the unique fashion in which flashbacks are employed but the humor exhibited in the characters' interactions and behavior that really entertains and engages. While the situations are often serious or even life changing – Jack and Rebecca lose one of their triplets at birth, Kevin wrecks his TV acting career with an onset rant, Kate's obesity haunts every moment of her life, and Randall is furious with the father who abandoned him at a fire station in infancy – the tone is never overly serious or dark. There's always a sense of fun or an aspect of basic human appeal in every scene: a simple, smart tactic that connects the audience with each moment in the story.

This approach is clear even in the first few pages of the pilot where a very pregnant Rebecca and a randy Jack lie in bed together …

```
Jack leans to her stomach, talks to his unborn children:

          JACK
    Hey, Fearsome Threesome! Do you three
    know how much I love your mother!? Do
    you even have any idea!?
```

Managing multiple-protagonist syndromes 89

Rebecca responds with bad ventriloquy as "the babies."

                REBECCA
           (baby voice)
We know, now shut up and let your fatass wife go to sleep.

                JACK
Oh no. Birthday tradition is birthday tradition.
           (still to babies)
Close your eyes in there, Kids. Daddy is about to do some terrible things to Mommy.

                REBECCA
Oh, there is no way in hell.

Jack, determined, tries kissing her neck.

                REBECCA (CONT'D)
           (amused)
How the hell can you possibly want me right now?

                JACK
In any state, my wife, you arouse me.

He kisses her neck more.

                REBECCA
I bet I can make that go away.

                JACK
Nothing you can say can –

                REBECCA
My water just broke.

Jack freezes. A beat, then …

                JACK
Yep.

In the very first scene we hear the distinct voices of the series' lead characters matched with a major plot point topped off with a touch of humor: all unexpected yet still accessible and believable; a consistent style visible in every moment of the pilot and the series that came thereafter. Needless to say, accomplishing this is no easy feat, especially when you factor in the plotting and production challenges of servicing a large ensemble cast, three diverse locations and two divergent timelines throughout every episode of the series.

In another scene, we see how unexpected yet believable character choices can properly and effectively propel a story. Through a private detective, Randall has hunted down William Hill, the biological father who abandoned him as infant. Instead of a familiar or clichéd interchange between an angry, defensive old man and an accusatory son, we witness a moment of sincere honesty and human decency.

>   WILLIAM (CONT'D)
> I'd like to say I remember your mom, but I barely do.
> Lived on the streets then. Crack, heroin. I remember her
> dying. Remember there was a baby. I'd like to say I remember
> leaving you at a fire station, but I don't. Not an excuse. In
> fact, it probably tells you something about me that I
> don't remember. I do like fire stations though, so that
> sounds like something I'd do if I had to do something,
> you know? Anyway, I don't know if that's what you're
> looking for, but either way, you can be sure this life
> of mine has been punishment enough for the things I've done.
>
>   RANDALL
> If you think I'm going to forgive you –
>
>   WILLIAM
> I don't.
>
>   RANDALL
> You were right, I did just want to say
> screw you and storm out of here.
>
>   WILLIAM
> Go 'head.
>
>   RANDALL
> Screw you.
>
>   WILLIAM
> Yep.
>
> Randall turns, storms out. A moment passes, he re-enters.
>
>   RANDALL
> You want to meet your grandchildren?
>
>   WILLIAM
> I'll get my coat.

We don't expect this sad old man, a father who abandoned his own baby, to be so open and honest in his own self-assessment of the most significant failure of his entire life. We also don't expect Randall to make the generous if rash choice to introduce this man to his own children. The scene not only works on a basic dramatic level, it speaks to one of the supplementary themes of the entire series – true forgiveness can profoundly service second chances.

Mention must also be made of some very smart decisions reached between the writing of this script and the production of the pilot. In the script, Randall tells William that his adoptive father "passed away a few years back." This line was cut in the broadcast episode, which facilitated Jack's unexpected and appalling death at the end of season two. When Jack and Rebecca adopt the infant Randall, they place the three babies in the bassinet with "The Fearsome Threesome" jumpers. This was changed to "The Big Three" in the pilot: which is simpler, more accessible and much more fun. In the scene in the hospital where we learn that the Jack and Rebecca timeline is actually set in the 1970s, dramatic details such as Nixon giving a speech on television, people smoking freely in a hospital, or the garish dress and hairstyles of the time – none of these are specifically delineated in the pilot script.

In the sequence where Kevin has his meltdown during the production of an episode of his abominable series *The Manny*, Ted Danson was originally scripted to play the actor playing his father. In the broadcast pilot, Alan Thicke performed the part with a much smarmier attitude than was indicated with Danson, which played beautifully within the context of this failed show within a good show. Another scene in the hospital where Doctor K tells Jack that one of his triplets has died ends with the doctor assuring Jack that the surviving babies will have a good father. In the script, the moment went on for two additional, redundant speeches. Edits and adjustments like this can have a major impact cumulatively on the end product. When in doubt, cut. Less is always more.

It should be noted that the same writer working with similar themes had considerable success in the feature comedy *Crazy Stupid Love* but was not nearly as successful in the dramatic feature *Life Itself*. Whether this pertains to the strictures and limitations offered by a drama as opposed to comedy or is simply proof of the adage that lightning never strikes twice in the same (creative) space, you be the judge. In any case, it is not unusual or necessarily unproductive for a writer to revisit similar themes, characters, and concepts. While practice may not make a story perfect it certainly offers creative opportunity.

A note on television dialogue

As can be seen in *This Is Us*, as in all film and television series, dialogue is the lifeblood of your script through which the drama, characters, themes, and plots all pump into the heart of your story. If the members of your ensemble don't speak with striking and authentic voices that differentiate as well as entertain, your characters will simply not engage the audience. But what if your world is so distinct in its environment, period, or the occupations of its characters that their language and attitudes must be clearly defined in an exceptional or unfamiliar manner?

In another ensemble drama, *Star Trek: The Next Generation* (1987–1994), DC not only needed to maintain the voices of an array of regular characters, he often had to write scenes which respected or mirrored the technical aspects of a 24th-century *Enterprise*. This "science," while not real, still had to be consistent and believable. This necessitated creating "technobabble" for specific scenes and circumstances that honored the pseudo-science that had already been established in previous episodes. In a post-Civil War western project like *Lazarus Man* (1996), DC researched the time and milieu to not only gain a grasp of an appropriate style of language for the characters but for key plot elements as well. In *Diagnosis Murder* (1993–2001), the writing of myriad emergency room and surgical scenes would have been impossible without the medical consultants that advised the creative staff of the show.

If there are any procedural or technical aspects to your series – whether it's a piece of science fiction set on the planet Venus or a blue-collar drama set in a Detroit gas station – get your nomenclature right. If you can't expend the effort to make the words you put into your characters' mouths authentic to their milieu or background, then don't waste your readers' time with any project of any scope or intention. You might as set your story in a generic apartment with a cast of bored and lonely people who have never maintained a job beyond trash collection (and, even then, wouldn't you want to know how the driver of a garbage truck really talks?).

All of these challenges burgeon and proliferate in an ensemble series. The more characters, the more voices. The more occupations and distinct environments, the more your people's language, jobs and attitudes need to be specifically addressed in their dialogue.

But even for an ensemble drama, the Showtime series *Billions* (2016–) is particularly ambitious. Its premise focuses on two sets of energetic, antagonistic characters – Bobby Axelrod or "Axe" and his family and co-workers headquartered out of his Axe Capital hedge fund, who are pitted in a life or death struggle against Charles "Chuck" Rhoades, Jr., US Attorney for the Southern District of New York, and his family, staff, and friends. With two distinct but overlapping worlds, each with their own nomenclature and vernacular, the writers of *Billions* must not only service multiple characters with their disparate story lines, they need to honor their diverse languages as well.

The challenge is continuous almost from scene to scene. Whether it's a legal moment like this one in the *Billions* pilot script, (written by Brian Koppelman, David Levien, and Andrew Ross Sorkin) between Axe and his lawyer …

>   HALL
> I checked with my sources in
> Washington, at the SEC and US
> Attorney's office. At this moment,

>   there's no case file, but Dan
>   Margolis was pinched. He was
>   released on his lawyer's
>   recognizance. Arraignment is
>   currently on hold.
>
>   AXE
>   Which tells you what.
>
>   HALL
>   That he's cooperating. How the hell
>   did you know?
>
>   AXE
>   He was making too much eye contact,
>   barely blinked, and his pulse was
>   hammering like he was running a
>   marathon. Suddenly I felt like I
>   did fourth quarter of 2007 when the
>   housing bubble was gonna burst and
>   only me and five other guys knew
>   it. So I called you.

Or an interchange dealing with finance …

>   DOPP
>   I had to pay in six hundred
>   thousand for my equity share. I
>   went into hock for that.
>
>   CONNERTY
>   Don't poor mouth yourself. A
>   million a year. Fordham Law schlub
>   makes good.
>
>   DOPP
>   (fork waving)
>   You do the math: Taxes. My million
>   turns into five hundred and change
>   before we even start. A hundred
>   grand a year on the mortgage and
>   maintenance for the apartment,
>   ninety grand for Jesse and Will to
>   go to Dalton. Summer camp. Alana
>   gets pregnant again, I'm working at
>   a car wash on weekends.

… you have to know your stuff.

You must also know your characters, of course. In a project like *Billions* this can be exceptionally demanding when you consider that the show's people are so consistently cold, relentless and merciless in the pursuit of their goals. A solid example of this methodology is visible in the first scene in the pilot where we meet Axe. As he orders a real estate agent to give him the premier shot at the purchase of a massive, palatial mansion, we witness his overweening ambition and desire to succeed, his inherent ruthlessness and insensitivity.

> AXE
> I'll take a seventy-two hour exclusive window. Show it to anyone else, I never think about it again. Prick should've shown me first.

As they get in the car.

> WAGS
> You really considering it? A buy like this will make a lot of noise.

> AXE
> Sometimes I like noise.

As the pilot proceeds and we meet the other characters going about their business in their various occupations or pursuits, we witness a uniform approach to all these people no matter what they're doing. In stark contrast to *This Is Us*, which offers use a world of universally decent and well-intentioned human beings – struggling to make their way through life in as compassionate a manner as they can, no matter their flaws, challenges or circumstances – the population of *Billions* is uniformly corrupt, fundamentally cruel and maniacally self-interested. These creatures are willing to commit any infraction, felony, or moral crime to achieve their immediate ends, even if it means betraying their own partners or family members.

This includes Chuck Rhoades, a US District Attorney, who is supposed to be upholding the law, not twisting it into a pretzel, which he is more than inclined to do. In a scene where his father, Senior, tries to get him to provide leniency for a man named Wolkowska, an old friend who has been convicted of financial crimes, Chuck brutally rebuffs and even threatens his parent.

> CHUCK
> My father always taught me that "mercy" was a word pussies used when they couldn't take the pain.

Wolkowska absorbs it. Senior shakes his head.

> SENIOR
> Maybe I taught you too well.

```
                    CHUCK
        I love you, dad, but if you walk
        into my office and try to use your
        influence again, you'll walk out of
        here in handcuffs.
```

To flip a famous speech in *The Godfather* when Michael Corleone says, "It's not personal Sonny, it's strictly business," in *Billions* it's never business, it's strictly personal. This defines every character in the series, providing a dark and consistent energy to the proceedings, which is why it works so well as an ensemble drama.

To sum up, as you approach the development of an ensemble television series, whether it's a compassionate, family-focused project like *This Is Us* or an exemplification of human greed and excess such as *Billions*, a coherent and stable slant on your characters, their personal code, and their manner of expressing themselves is as important as the development of your world, themes, and scenario.

What did we learn?

Ensemble projects can involve multiple characters and storylines that are linked in some fashion.
Episodic stories are not necessarily directly linked outside of a general premise or concept.
Ensemble can play with time.
Ensemble can play with location.
The ensemble anchor character can tie the various elements of an ensemble story together.
Narrative urgency, character conflict, and plot progression are as important in an ensemble piece as in any other kind of story.
Ensemble works especially well in television where multiple characters and storylines can provide narrative support for multiple seasons. But, even more than in traditional series, due diligence must be applied to developing and consistently maintaining the characters' voices, plotlines, and environments.

Exercise

Write three premises. In the first, create a geographic ensemble piece where at least five characters are interconnected but inhabiting different locales. Bring them together by the end of the story as it climaxes in a particular location. In the second premise, create an ensemble anchor for your story that connects or bridges the characters. This piece can be set in either multiple locations or a single locale. In the third premise, create a single-location piece with no ensemble anchor with multiple characters and point of views. Make at least one of these premises a genre piece – a horror, mystery, thriller, or science-fiction story.

Now turn one of these premises into a television pilot concept, which entails continuing storylines and characters as opposed to a single, finite plot line

Then, just for fun, take any story you happen to be working on and turn it into an ensemble piece if it isn't already. By the end of this exercise, you should have at least one interesting ensemble idea.

9 Based on true events and research

Ever hear about something and say, "Wow! That would make a great movie!"? There was a screenwriter, under commission by a German television production company that had found Ann Franks' childhood best friend and wanted a screenplay written before she passed away. The writer interviewed the woman, did extensive research and then started writing the script. But the notes she got back from the company were all from the old woman who kept saying things like, "That's not how it actually happened, that's not what we really did and that's not what we talked about." So the writer kept changing it to be more "authentic" and the screenplay became more and more mundane. After several drafts the project was dropped and the inspirational moments of that friendship are now lost forever.

When we write a "true story" we need to keep in mind that drama outweighs truth. We can't allow ourselves, as writers, to become locked into what "really happened." Rather, we need to be faithful to the emotional truth rather than the historical truth.

Adapting history

Seabiscuit (2003), screenplay by Gary Ross, wouldn't be an inspiring story that transcends time if it were simply locked into the bare truth. Based on the real Depression-era racehorse and the three men who needed a second chance who came together to make racing history, Ross stayed as close to the historic facts as he could, but did not hesitate to fictionalize elements in order to raise dramatic tension and further our emotional connections with the three central characters.

Tom Smith, the horse trainer, was a strange, socially ostracized cowboy at the time millionaire Charles Howard hired him. But how they actually met is irrelevant compared to how Ross has them meet and connect. In Ross's version, Howard sees Smith taking care of a lame horse out in the wilderness. In this, one of the many great scenes of the screenplay, Howard visits Smith in the brush late at night to ask him why he is tending to a racehorse that will never be able to race again. In this scene the truth of the entire story, the theme if you will, is revealed by Smith: "You don't throw away a whole life just cause it's banged up a little."

The scene probably never took place. Why would Smith camp out in the brush anyway? The truth is – who cares? This moment works better this way than however they really met; it reveals character for both these men and does so in a dramatic and cinematic way. This scene rings true emotionally and sets up the theme that will be repeated several times in several different ways throughout the picture.

Another great scene is when Smith tries to get a jockey to ride the less-than-tame Seabiscuit only to have the horse bite a piece of his shirt off. Several stable hands attempt to hold down the wild and bucking horse as Smith turns away. But the next vision that Smith, as well as the audience, shares is to witness the too-large jockey Red fighting off several men in a different section of the stables. The comparison is obvious to Smith and the audience. The two are a natural fit. The scene is fun and humors us. Did it happen? It seems too contrived to be real, and indeed it is but does it work dramatically? Absolutely. Yes, Red did try to earn money in small-time boxing matches, but was he really so ill-tempered that he got into fights all the time? If he were always in fights while working at the racetrack, isn't it likely that the track owners would have fired him? Does any of this matter? Again, absolutely not. It works and is true emotionally to the story, if not to history.

One of the most obvious departures from historic fact that makes the screenplay so effective is its ending. After both the jockey and the horse suffer broken legs, they make a comeback to win the Santa Anita Handicap, which they had lost years ago. That is both the historic and dramatic truth. Powerful. But if the film ended with them riding easily to victory, or even gradually moving up through the pack, it would be anti-climactic.

What Ross does is to take great dramatic license and have Seabiscuit and Red both struggling with their pain and falling well behind. It is his friend and fellow jockey Georgie who drops back on his horse to ask how they are doing that adds a personal touch and helps serve the emotional truth we are all waiting for. Ross has well established that Seabiscuit runs the fastest after he looks another horse in the eye. It is his sense of competition that makes him a winner; this seems to stem from the historic facts. Now Ross plays with the facts and has Georgie provide his ailing friend with the needed push that will send them into an amazing comeback. He gives Seabiscuit another horse to look in the eye. The result is a great emotional moment when both Seabiscuit and Red bite the bullet and bolt into history – coming from behind to first place.

This is the true story of Seabiscuit: that the underdog can be a winner, and that you don't give up on a whole life just because it's banged up a little. Nothing could illustrate this more than the fictionalized finale. Dramatic license is something all writers are given without a permit. We should not hesitate to use it, for it can help lead us to the finish line as well.

Another example is *Argo* (2012), written by Chris Terrio, based on the May 2007 *Wired* magazine article entitled "The Great Escape" by Joshuah Bearman; and chapter nine of the book entitled "The Master of Disguise" by

Antonio Mendez, is a dramatization of the escape of six US diplomats from Tehran during the Iranian hostage crisis in 1979–1981. This movie, which is a mix of adventure film, hostage drama, and supposedly true-life events, ends with Antonio Mendez, a CIA operative, spiriting the diplomats out of the country in a Swissair DC-10 just moments before a squad of Komiteh, or Iranian Revolutionary Guards, rush down the runway in jeeps in a frantic and vain attempt to capture them.

```
INT. SWISSAIR DC-10 - MORNING

Mendez looking out the window -

EXT. AIRPORT RUNWAY - MORNING

ANGLE ON THE THREE IRANIAN VEHICLES

speeding ahead - they're GAINING ON us -

INT. COCKPIT - CONTINUOUS ACTION

The CO-PILOT looks out the window. Sees they are being
pursued by militia and police. He looks to the Pilot.

A beat. The Pilot reaches down and pushes all four
engines to go FULL THROTTLE.

EXT. AIRPORT RUNWAY - CONTINUOUS ACTION

ANGLE ON THE JEEPS

We start to PULL AWAY FROM them - leaving them behind -
beginning to RISE UP -
```

This is a classic movie cliffhanger – anxiety-inducing, heart-pounding, and intensely dramatic. Considering *Argo*'s entire structure has been built to climax with this riveting resolution, it's exactly the right ending for this film. The problem is, it didn't happen. In reality, the six diplomats just boarded a plane to Zurich without any interference or threat from anyone and simply flew away. But that would have made for a lousy ending to a geopolitical suspense thriller, which is what *Argo* was designed to be. Ending the film without some kind of cliffhanger just simply wouldn't have functioned for the audience.

Free yourself from the truth

Another excellent example is *Catch Me if You Can* (2002). Jeff Nathanson's screenplay is based on the autobiography of con-artist and check forger

Frank Abagnale. Frank was a teenager when he became one of the most resourceful, creative and successful con-artists in the 1960s. While this could easily be a psychological crime drama or a comedy caper film, Nathanson's skill in expanding on the truth allowed him to find the emotional truth – in a tale of neglect, abandonment and loneliness. In *Catch Me if You Can*, Nathanson developed a story of a boy who is desperate to find a place where he belongs and a relationship where he can be himself.

The story begins with FBI agent Carl coming to a French prison to extradite Frank. The prison conditions are horrendous and Frank is sick and weak. Carl attempts to remain all business, but can't help feeling compassion for his prisoner and insisting on a doctor. In reality, Frank did serve time in a French prison. But he also served time in prisons in two other countries as well. Including that in the screenplay would be redundant and only the French prison had such horrible conditions.

To offset this darkness, Nathanson preludes the screenplay with a segment of the old TV show "To Tell the Truth," on which Frank really was a guest. This helps to establish the film's true tone, that of a game. After the prison scene, Nathanson sends us into the past and reveals the falling apart of Frank's home life. As we have noted earlier, he gives us the first insight into Frank's personality when his parents are called into the high school principal's office and are told their truly brilliant son has shanghaied some teacher's French class.

Whether this really happened or not doesn't matter. What is important is that this scene establishes Frank's bold character, setting the tone for the rest of the story. Audiences love to root for the underdog, especially one who beats the system. This is the character Nathanson skillfully sets up in his writing, but he adds a troubled soul in with the mix, making Frank a more three-dimensional character. This is no light subject. *Catch Me if You Can* is a story of a boy pretending to be a man in order to steal to survive – a boy who gets no guidance whatsoever from his parents, who are only concerned with themselves.

Nathanson re-introduces Carl, the FBI agent, 20 minutes after we first saw him, as the antagonist who hunts down Frank. But Carl will also fill the void left by Frank's father. Carl becomes the only man who really cares about Frank, and in a way, Frank gives Carl something as well. These characters are set up as opposites – Frank the freewheeling, anything-goes, fun-loving young con-artist and Carl, the mature, deadpan, ultra-serious workaholic. What they both share is a loneliness that Nathanson reveals beautifully by having Frank call up Carl at the FBI offices on Christmas eve. To hammer home the significance of the situation, Nathanson even has Frank tell Carl exactly where he is staying. But Carl, alone in the office with a photo of his ex-wife and child, refuses to believe him. This is such a skillfully written scene that it skips over being manipulative and moves into melancholy. Did it ever really happen?

In reality, the FBI agent who did catch Frank didn't start searching for him from the beginning of Frank's career. He never had contact with him. No phone calls on Christmas, no game of cat and mouse. Nathanson creates this, just as Nathanson adds in several scenes with Frank trying to reconnect with his father, and Carl meeting Frank's father. In reality, Frank never saw his father after his parents broke up and the FBI agent never did either.

Nathanson's script plays with reality, exchanging the truth for what is more dramatic and better fits the theme and the story arc. The inventions Nathanson adds are believable and totally within the tone and context of the true story.

Was the real Frank upset with the tampering of his life story? Not at all. Is it a lie to the audience? Okay, maybe, but so what? Aren't all movies a lie in the first place? They didn't really shoot the film in the 1960s and those aren't the real people, they're famous actors. But the story, tone and emotional experience remain true to the heart of Frank's true experience.

So if you find yourself writing about a true event, keep in mind that when the story benefits from keeping it the way it really happened, that's great. But when a few changes, or even stretches of the truth, will serve the dramatic story better and make a deeper connection with your audience, free yourself from the truth by all means.

Another superb example of getting to the truth about something in the past without being overly burdened by it is the mix of fictional and non-fictional elements in *I, Tonya*, written by Steven Rogers. This radical hybrid of absurd mockumentary and intensely felt sports drama shouldn't function as well as it does but its singular focus on its lead character's journey pulls us along. While we swing from staged talking head interviews of Tonya Harding and her ex-husband, to over-the-top moments where she breaks the fourth wall, to skating scenes in a variety of colorful venues, to dramatic exchanges in courtrooms and trailer parks, we never lose track of what the film is really about. A few lines from a single scene between Tonya and her Gorgon of a mother make this point as loud as a gunshot.

               TONYA
Did you ever love me? Or anything
even?

Lavona is momentarily thrown. But she recovers quickly. Then:

               LAVONA
You think Sonja Henie's mother loved
her? Poor fuckin' you. I didn't stay
home making Apple Brown Bettys. No I
made you a champion! Knowing you'd hate
me for it. That's the sacrifice a
mother makes. I wish I had a mother
like me. Instead of nice. Nice gets

```
          you shit. I didn't like my mother
          either. So what? I gave you a gift.

Tonya stands, faces Lavona. Before she walks away:

               TONYA
          You cursed me. You're a monster.

               LAVONA
          Spilled milk, baby.
```

Moments like this that explains why the bizarre amalgam of genres that provides the foundation for *I, Tonya* work together so effortlessly. At its heart, this is a story about an ill-treated, talented, and determined young woman who managed to persevere and achieve some semblance of her goals despite a heartless mother, an abusive husband, and a dismissive skating world. As Tonya tries, fails, tries, and ultimately fails, the shifts in time, format, and genre only enhance a story that, if it had been told in a more traditional manner, would have been far less engaging and unanticipated. Is it true or is it mostly fictional or fictionalized? Who cares? It's a good movie.

Find a special event in history

All of the examples we'll be addressing in this chapter, no matter the time, place, or period, have one thing in common – their stories hadn't been told. Despite all the many TV series and films produced on myriad historical subjects, there's still 10,000 years of recorded human history to work with and there's always something old that can be made into something new; a new story, that is.

The American space program has been heavily chronicled in film and television, literally *From the Earth to the Moon*, to *Apollo 13*, to *The Right Stuff* and so on. Understandably the vast majority of these projects focus on the astronauts that took the great risk of going into space and achieving great things. But what about the people back on Earth at NASA who helped them get their spacecraft off the ground to they could go into space in the first place?

Hidden Figures (2016), screenplay by Allison Schroeder and Theodore Melfi, based on the book *Hidden Figures* by Margot Shetterly, dramatizes the story of three African American women – Katherine Goble Johnson, Dorothy Vaughn, and Mary Jackson – who, in various ways, provided critical mathematical support for the launch of Mercury 7 in 1962. The story works on two levels; one, the challenges and mechanics of the work itself; and two, the barriers these women of color had to hurdle to gain the position and respect they needed to complete that work despite the segregated mores of the time. As we watch these women achieve their goals despite all the obstacles, both societal and professional, thrown their way, the very premise of this story is rife with the stuff that makes fascinating historical drama. Only in a period piece set in the Jim Crow south could we have a moment that dramatizes the astonishing stupidity of separate but equal bathroom facilities when Katherine's supervisor asks her why she's always away in the bathroom. Her response functions at the highest level of plot, commentary, and drama.

> KATHERINE
> There's no bathroom for me here.
>
> AL HARRISON
> There's no bathroom? What do you mean there's no bathroom for you here?

Katherine can't take it anymore. Her voice rises.

> KATHERINE
> There's no bathroom here. There are no COLORED bathrooms in this building or ANY building outside the West Campus. Which is half a mile away! Did you know that? I have to walk to Timbuktu just to relieve myself! And I can't take one of the handy bikes. Picture that, with my uniform: skirt below the knees and my heels. And don't get me started about the "simple pearl necklace" I can't afford. Lord knows you don't pay "the coloreds" enough for that. And I work like a dog day and night, living on coffee from a coffee pot half of you don't want me to touch! So excuse me if I have to go to the restroom a few times a day!

You can hear a pin drop. Katherine takes her purse, personals and walks off. Leaving everyone's jaws on the ground.

This is perhaps the film's strongest scene; one that serves character, suits the period, and meets audience expectations. However, this never happened. The real Katherine Goble Johnson simply ignored the separate but equal facilities and went to any bathroom she liked. But it's hard to see how *Hidden Figures* could have worked without this scene, a believable invention.

Find a special place in history

If there is a historical period that provides more narrative fodder for film and television than any other, it's probably World War II. What other event offers writers such clearly defined heroes and villains locked in such a ferocious, bloody battle over the freedom of the entire world? That terrible and dramatic time between 1939 and 1945 is ripe for exploitation. The problem is, every day, week, and month of those years has already been mined to the bottom of its shaft from almost every conceivable angle, in every theater of the war, from all sides of this great conflict. If a writer is going to tackle this place in history, they need to find a story, or at least a take on a story, that hasn't been told to death. Of course, this would be the case for any historical subject but particularly one as well as explored as World War II.

The Darkest Hour (2017), written by Anthony McCarten, focuses on Winston Churchill as he became Prime Minister of Britain in 1940 while the Germans were launching their ultimately successful invasion of Western Europe. Churchill is one of the best-known historical figures of the war and certainly one of the most dramatized in films and television. We're all familiar with his distinctive character, voice, courage and persistence and of what a great political and military leader he was.

But do we know that his own Conservative party did not want him to be Prime Minister? That he was almost broke at the beginning of the war? That he was isolated and unsupported in his determination to fight and defeat Hitler? That the King of England didn't want him? That his responsibility for the disastrous invasion of Gallipoli in World War I and his reputation as a heavy drinker drew jeers from his peers?

In fact, there were strong elements within his own War Cabinet who wished to make peace with Hitler and leave Europe to the tender mercies of the Nazis. This point is made abundantly clear in a powerful scene in the House of Commons as Churchill makes a passionate speech in a vain attempt to convince his people to fight the Germans.

INT. COMMONS/ PARLIAMENT – DAY

ANGLE ON: ERNLE HASTINGS, unable to take his eyes off CHAMBERLAIN, waiting for the HANDKERCHIEF to be waved.

ANGLE ON WINSTON: readying himself for the final assault!

          WINSTON
We have before us an ordeal of the
most grievous kind. We have before
us many, many long months of
struggle and of suffering. You ask,
what is our policy? I say it is to
wage war by sea, land and air, with
all our might and with all the
strength God can give us—to wage
war against a monstrous tyranny
never surpassed in the dark and

```
          lamentable catalogue of human
          crime.

ANGLE ON: HALIFAX, in the GALLERY - he shoots a look to
CHAMBERLAIN.

                    WINSTON (CONT'D)
          That is our policy. You ask, what
          is our aim? I can answer in one
          word. Victory - victory at all
          costs, victory in spite of terror,
          victory however long and hard the
          road may be. For without victory,
          there is no survival.

WINSTON feels he must have won them over, but his confident
smile fades as he realizes he stands alone.

Small KNUCKLE-KNOCKING begins - but it is MUTED.

SIMON and HOARE and the other CONSERVATIVE PLOTTERS all look
to CHAMBERLAIN, as he -

- puts his WHITE HANDKERCHIEF back in his BREAST POCKET!!!

The TORIES sit back - NONE APPLAUD.
```

In the course of this story not only does Churchill face fierce opposition from Halifax, Chamberlain, and other people in his own Cabinet, he makes crucial mistakes. He lies to the British people, assuring them the situation in France is far less dire than it actually is; he amazes the French when he insists, with their army in full retreat, that they counter-attack. He browbeats his new secretary to tears and smokes and drinks as much as he breathes. This all makes for a fresh and engrossing take on this revered character, knocking him off his historical pedestal in almost every scene in the script until finally, through sheer grit, piss and verve, the man turns the situation around and literally saves England.

As with the other examples we've explored, the writer McCarten took some liberties with the truth. Much attention is paid to the British soldiers based in Calais who hindered the German advance on Dunkirk but no mention is made of the far more important defensive work done by the French troops fighting outside the town. A pivotal scene where Winston traveled on the Underground to gage the mood of average Britons actually never happened. A radio speech he makes from the House of Commons would have been technologically impractical at the time. But none of this matters; what does matter is making good drama from a piece of the truth, not literally recording it; that's for documentaries. To quote a line from *The Man Who Shot Liberty Valance*, "When the legend becomes fact, print the legend."

Another excellent example of this is *The Revenant* (2015), written by Mark L. Smith and Alejandro G. Iñárritu, based on the novel by Michael Punke. Supposedly based on an incident in 1823 when a trapper, Hugh Glass, was left for dead in the wilds of North America after a brutal grizzly bear attack, the film focuses on his relentless drive to survive as he drags himself across hundreds of rugged miles to seek bloody revenge on the men who abandoned him and killed his half-Pawnee son. The problem historically is that Glass may have never made the trek he described in the first place, he was a notorious fabricator of tales, and he certainly didn't kill the men who left him behind; he only wanted the gun they had taken from him. But the truth would have made for a lousy movie while the "reinvention" of the story produced an excellent film – partly because the story had not been widely told.

The most important lesson here is that, when exploring history, find some piece of it that no one has found before and dig into that vein of gold as deep as you can.

Research that works for you

When we write period pieces, we need to do the research as to what the time period was like, how did they talk, what was the normal form of existence at the time. The trick is being able to convey these elements without boring our audience with a history lecture. Marc Norman and Tom Stoppard's screenplay for *Shakespeare in Love* (1998) demonstrates that something can be historically correct and still be much more than a history channel segment or a period romance novel. They managed to make us feel like we were actually there in that moment, and not just learning about it. The dialogue is only partially affected towards the time period and some more anachronistic situations, such as the moment when the taxi boat driver hands Will his own play (everyone has a play or a screenplay don't they?), help us identify with the characters and their lives.

Norman and Stoppard literally pull out the stops on the literary history of perhaps the world's most famous playwright, William Shakespeare. What is truly striking is how fluidly they slip in historic facts surrounding the Bard and his time, incorporating them into the story for both plot and just great effects. These men have done their homework. Within the first 5 minutes, while still setting up the time, place and status quo of the story, Norman and Stoppard reveal some of the gems of their research and how well they will employ it throughout the film.

The film opens with theater producer Henslowe's feet being held in a fire by the two henchmen of Fennyman, the moneylender. When Henslowe promises to have the money in 3 weeks, Fennyman has his feet removed from the fire and is asked how.

```
              HENSLOWE
    I have a wonderful new play.
```

                    FENNYMAN
          Put his feet in.

                    HENSLOWE
          It's a comedy.

                    FENNYMAN
          Cut his nose off.

                    HENSLOWE
          A new comedy by William Shakespeare.

                    FENNYMAN
          And his ears.

Norman and Stoppard use this simple exchange not only for comedic effect, but to establish the standing of Shakespeare in Elizabethan society and the state of theater in general. Theater was a lowly profession located, as the writers display in the film, between brothels and taverns. Shakespeare himself was a mere freelance writer, dashing off whatever he could sell. The moral distaste for drama is presented blatantly by page 8 when Will passes a preacher on the street decrying the corrupting influences of theater to any and all. This character will reappear, literally pulled into the theater by the end of the film and enraptured by the first performance of *Romeo and Juliet*. But the writers give him more importance than just this fun little gag of setup and pay-off; they offer us a glimpse of the place or places from which Will gets his poetry. For as the preacher spouts on, condemning the two theaters of the neighborhood, the Curtain and the Rose, he shouts, as Will passes by: "And the Rose smells thusly rank by any name. A plague on both their houses." Will takes notice of the phrases – which we know he will rewrite and make immortal.

Another wonderful example of the writer's use of historic elements is the simple and underlying subplot of the rivalry between Will and Christopher Marlowe. While we only see Marlowe once, his plays are always mentioned and the actors all audition for Will using a Marlowe monologue. The present-day academic debate as to whether Marlowe may have written some of Will's plays provides the basis of the wonderful bar scene between the two playwrights as Marlowe gives Will advice on the play he is trying to write, *Romeo and Ethel*, suggesting changes that become the very backbone of *Romeo and Juliet*. One cannot write reference humor if one doesn't know the reference, and the humor here works regardless of whether you are aware of the academic arguments or not.

The writers utilize other wonderful and intriguing facts from the past, enlisting them into the plots, subplots and comedy of the screenplay, making them more than passing period color, but essential plot points. The fact that women could not perform on stage, that Queen Elizabeth loved theater, even the fact that Will only wrote whatever he thought would sell, become wonderful undercurrents which frame the story and provide much of the conflict. While this story as to how Shakespeare came to write his most famous play may be entirely fictional, by making the story's world and plot elements true to history, Norman and Stoppard crafted a heart- and mind-winning portrait of William Shakespeare, bringing him down off the exalted pedestal scholars have placed him on and allowing him to walk among the rest of us as a hardworking, very human, run-of-the-mill romantic with a gift and love for his art.

This all applies to television

Of course you have history displayed in a host of television series as diverse as *Outlander*, *Mad Men*, *Downton Abbey*, and *That '70s Show*. Needless to say it's much harder to produce history properly on a television budget and schedule, but amazing things can still be done. Look at *The Empty Child* (2005), the first episode of the recent reinvention of the inimitable *Doctor Who* (2005–) written by Stephen Moffat (the series' eventual show runner). During the London Blitz, a little boy in a gas mask hunts through the streets of the bombed out city, asking people, "Are you my mummy?" As he wanders about, he spreads an alien contagion that turns everyone he meets into a mindless creature with a gas mask growing across his or her faces. Only when Doctor Who realizes this cursed little boy needs to embrace his actual mother is the crisis averted and all the victims returned to normal. In this, one of the best *Doctor Who* episodes, we have science fiction, history, and drama all combined together into a satisfying whole. This is an example of cross genre, which we will examine more extensively in Chapter 10. But the key element in *The Empty Child* is history – drastically transformed and reconstituted to suit the series' franchise – but history nonetheless.

This all applies to everything you write

Even if your piece is not set in London during the Blitz, or 1880s California, or 1940s New Jersey, you must do your research. In a contemporary crime thriller, the criminals and police will act and speak a certain way. In a hospital drama, your medical jargon must be accurate. A legal thriller will make no sense if you don't understand the law involved. And even if you set a story in a flower shop, you need to know what a casket piece is, how your shop's owner would use Teleflora, and what his turnaround on a corsage might be.

To sum up, research is essential in almost anything we write. Often through research we can find intriguing elements that make the story feel all the more authentic. And when that happens, it connects with the audience in an even more special way. But the drama always takes precedent over the facts. "When the legend becomes fact, print the legend."

What did we learn?

Always do your research.
Learn the facts, then throw them out when it suits you. Print the legend.
This all applies to television.

Exercise

For this exercise you will write three scenes, all of which will require some level of research.

For the first scene, pick a historical event that fascinates you; one that hopefully contains fascinating people as well. Focus on a moment in that event that could have taken place between two of those people in a confined or simple location. Research not only the facts of the incident but also the language, dress and customs of the time. Now write that scene as accurately to the period and its people as you can.

Now choose a procedural or highly skilled environment you are not familiar with; such as a police station, operating room, nuclear lab, etc. Research the nomenclature, jargon, dress, props, and other pertinent details of that environment. Create a pair of characters that are working in this world and now write a dramatic scene between the two of them as accurately as you can.

Now write a scene based on your own family background, going back at least a generation. Pick two people from your family during an interesting time, research the jargon, dress, props, and other pertinent details of their environment, and write a dramatic scene.

10 Set-up, pay-off and the twist

Anton Chekhov said that if you show a gun in the first act it has to be used by the last one. Chekhov was describing *set-up and pay-off*, a common device well used in mysteries and thrillers but employable in almost any genre. After all, what is a joke other than a set-up with the punchline as the pay-off?

Why use set-up and pay-off? Have you ever heard people say, "Everything happens for a reason?" or "What goes around comes around?" There seems to be a universal belief that all humans share that there is a reason for things and that some justification can be found in almost anything – a belief in a karmic set-up and pay-off. When it's placed in your screenplay, it feeds this universal hunger, which can provide a sense of fullness and completion for your audience.

What are set-up and a pay-off in their simplest form? A set-up is the installation of a piece of information, a prop, or even a talent or knowledge possessed by a character which will come into play in a major way, having a dramatic effect on the story, generally during the third act. If the pay-off happens at the end of the third act, it's regarded as a "twist ending." There can be several set-ups and pay-offs throughout the story. Ones that dramatically alter the story are called plot twists. Sometimes these twists can arrive without a set-up, and these generally appear to come out of the blue. Audiences react to them as, "Where'd that come from?" Poorly constructed or placed set-ups and plot twists are generally considered not only unsatisfactory but downright irritating. But when done correctly, audiences love the curves in the highway.

Let's say that at the beginning of a story a character is trying to fix a banister that's loose at the top of a long flight of stairs. We know that, by the end of the film, someone is going to lean on that banister and tumble to his or her death. Most probably this will happen during a climactic fight scene with a bad guy. For another example, let's say it's established in a story's first act that one character needs work done on his car's brakes. Obviously, at some point in the second or third act, someone will race off in the car and, lo and behold, the brakes will fail. If either of these examples had no set-up, if, during the course of the plot, someone discovered that the car had no brakes, or the banister just gave way for no reason, the action would be unbelievable and come out of left field. It'll piss people off.

Set-up, pay-off and the twist   111

The art of the set-up and the pay-off is to not tip your hand too early, or, even better, not at all. The set-up needs to be inserted in such a subtle way that, when the pay-off comes, the audience doesn't expect it but loves you for it. Mysteries are generally very good at this. The clue to unraveling the plot is exposed early on, but so much information and so many motives and possibilities eventually surface that the original clue is long overlooked and forgotten. If, however, the damning piece of evidence or information is not set up properly, the audience feels cheated. Mystery writers know their plots have worked well when, during the finale, the audience responds with a resounding "Oh, of course. I should have thought of that!" They haven't worked at all when the audience responds "Hold on! Who would have thought of that?"

It must be noted that your set-ups and pay-offs needn't be elaborate or complicated; they can be as simple as a comic or dramatic runner based on a single line or idea. A superb example of this is available in Billy Wilder and I. A.L. Diamond's script for *Some Like It Hot* (1959) where the lead characters are constantly referring to "type O" blood. The substance of an entire character in *Guardians of the Galaxy* is defined by the variety of ways he can say his name "Groot." And no one who has ever seen *Jaws* will ever forget the references to "a bigger boat."

The Twilight Zone set-up/pay-off

Setup and pay-off are not exclusive to the mystery and thriller genre. Rod Serling's *The Twilight Zone* (1959–1964) was famous for its set-up and pay-off twist endings. In the episode "One for the Angels" (1959), Serling presents us with Lew Bookman, a sidewalk salesman who has led a humble and uneventful life – until the day Death visits him and tells the man he must depart with him at midnight. The only way Lew can stay alive is to convince Death that he has some unfinished business: something important that he has yet to accomplish as his contribution to mankind. Lew, who gives away many of the toys he sells to the kids of the neighborhood, tells Death he has never made a really big pitch – a pitch for the angels. Death grants him his stay but then elects to take someone else at midnight. A car hits a little girl from the neighborhood and Death comes to the tenement just before midnight to claim her. Desperate to save the child, Lew greets Death on the building's steps and eloquently and intensely sells him a few ties and other meaningless items he presents as fabulous beyond belief, keeping Death from the little girl's door through one pitch after another. Of course, Death misses his midnight appointment, but Lew willingly goes along with him to the afterworld, having finally made that one great pitch – a pitch for the angels.

In this almost leisurely paced 30-minute TV episode, Serling sets up one pay-off after another. For example, when Death visits Lew, the little girl stops by his apartment. Lew, not believing Death is who he says he is, introduces the girl to the dark-suited figure. Not being able to see Death, she thinks it's a joke. Death states that only those who are about to go with him can see him. Why throw this scene in? Because, after the car hits the girl, and Lew rushes to her in the street, she asks Lew who that man in the dark suit is – and she points at Death.

This illustrates the truism that nothing should be placed in a script unless it has some kind of meaning or story value that furthers the characters or the story. The girl's earlier visit appeared to be extraneous. We already knew Lew liked children and saw him give toys to the girl and some other kids on the street, so why throw in her little visit? Why reveal that only those that are to go with Death can see him? These moments are all interesting, but unnecessary – unless we realize they're set-ups for something that will propel the story forward later in the plot. And they are.

Twist ending set-up/pay-offs

Perfect examples of excellent extended set-ups are present in movies like *Psycho, Get Out, Gone Girl, Chinatown, The Others* and *The Sixth Sense*, where the entire plot concept is built on a twist-ending pay-off. In *The Sixth Sense* (1999), writer/director M. Night Shyamalan reveals the set-up for his twist ending within the first 10 minutes. We actually see Malcolm (Bruce Willis) killed. But then the film switches to Malcolm following and then talking to a young boy with a truly unique and deep psychological problem – the poor kid sees dead people. The audience is led to believe that Malcolm has recovered physically from the shooting and is now on a journey to recover emotionally as well, by helping this stricken little boy. Shyamalan is careful and precise in the construction of every scene. No one except the boy ever talks to Malcolm. We never see anyone acknowledge Malcolm, even to the extent of opening a door for him. All the facts, all the clues, have been given to us upfront and so obviously that we fail to see them. The young boy even tells us what's up at one point (in a speech that has practically become an English idiom) when he cries, "I see dead people," adding that they don't even know they're dead. Shyamalan is honest with his mystery, laying out his story in a sensible fashion that is consistent and fair to his audience. When it is finally revealed at the end of the film that Malcolm is actually dead like all the other ghosts in the little boy's world, it comes as a shocking twist – but one the audience not only readily accepts but admires and adores.

Character, character, character

The best set-ups and twists are built on character. Agatha Christie constructed amazing mystery plots with astonishing twists and turns but her stories are rarely produced any longer because her characters are so thin, familiar and generic (the recent remake of *Murder on the Orient Express* is a prime example.) The main reason *The Sixth Sense* works so well is because the story is focused on two tormented people the audience can identify with and care about. No matter how convoluted, over the top, and high-concept the set-up/twist film may be, never lose sight of your characters. Make sure they generate the action of the plot rather than the other way around.

Set-up, pay-off and the twist

Look at *Get Out* (2017), written by Jordan Peele. What appears to be a character story about a young African American male, Chris, meeting his fiancée Rose's family quickly turns into a tale of terror with elements that would comfortably fit into Mary Shelley's *Frankenstein*. However, Peele (who has called his film a documentary as opposed to a science-fiction/horror thriller) is much more interested in a realistic theme he has certainly experienced in his own life – how does a black male survive in a white America while still maintaining his dignity and sanity? The ending, in which a police car arrives just after Chris has almost strangled his murderous, treacherous fiancée, says it all.

```
Siren lights flash on the side of their heads. The scene doesn't
look good. Chris turns towards them raising his hands. Rose
smiles again and pleads with the approaching officers.

                    ROSE
          Help. Help! He's trying to kill me.

The driver of the car opens the door. It's Rod. The sirens
are coming from a TSA security vehicle!

                    ROD
          Oh shit! Chris!
              (to Rose)
          You fucked now, huh?

Chris hobbles to the car. He gets in the passengers side. The
gravity of what he's been through sets in. Rod looks at
Chris. Rod tries to gage Chris's mental state… Chris is silent
and emotionless. Not a smirk. Rod realizes he may be too late
to save Chris's sanity. Rod looks at Rose through the
windshield.

                    ROD (CONT'D)
          What about her?

                    CHRIS
          I think we need some time apart.

Chris looks at Rod and gives a little smirk. Rod exhales in
relief. Rod does a three-point turn. Rod and Chris drive away
leaving Rose to die.

                    ROD
          I told you to get the fuck out that
          house, man.

Rose watches the car leave.
```

In *Gone Girl* (2014), screenplay by Gillian Flynn, based on her novel, the characters are a tormented and unhappy married couple, Nick and Amy Dunne. As the story begins with Amy's disappearance, it's quickly and believably established that Nick could have killed her and stashed her body somewhere. But then we learn she staged her disappearance to frame her husband. Twist after twist follows as the pressure builds in the story on Nick, who is fighting to stay out of jail while Amy lives a dark life on the run. After Nick appears to offer a heartfelt plea to the media her for her return, Amy decides to rejoin him, going so far as to commit a murder to enable their reunion. But even after all of these plot shenanigans, nothing matches the final, most unexpected but still credible twist in the story – Amy is pregnant with Nick's baby and they're going to build a family together.

```
ON TV: We see outtakes of the ELLEN ABBOTT interview.

          NICK
After so much darkness we have come
out united. We communicate. We are
honest. We're partners in crime.

          AMY
And Ellen, I'm happy to announce on
your show: soon we'll be parents.

ELLEN yelps with joy. AMY and ELLEN hug across NICK.

INT. BEDROOM - NIGHT

They lie down side by side on the marital bed. Nick is staring
at the back of Amy's head, just as in the opening.

          NICK (O.S.)
What are you thinking? How are you
feeling? What have we done to each
other? What will we do?

Amy turns, and gives him a haunting SMILE.
                                              FADE TO BLACK.
```

Not only is this climax a devastating one dramatically, it illustrates the entire film's main theme – that even the most brutal betrayal between a married couple can contain a twisted but still intense connection and intimacy. But it wouldn't have worked if it hadn't been so carefully set up early in the story just how cruelly and hopelessly intertwined Amy and Nick are in their bizarre marriage. The best set-ups and twists are built out of character; especially the misbegotten ones. Broken people can make for the best characters.

Twists in TV

Creating set-ups and plot twists is a staple of television, particularly in genre projects. The basic approach is the same, if foreshortened due to time and plot purposes. DC and his co-writer J. Larry Carroll successfully engineered a series of satisfying plot twists in *Future Imperfect* (1990), their episode of *Star Trek: The Next Generation* (1987–1994). In this story, Commander William T. Riker joins his colleagues on an away team mission to an isolated planet near the Neutral Zone, a restricted area in space designed to separate the United Federation of planets from the unfriendly Romulan Empire. As mysterious fumes gas Riker in a cave, he quickly loses consciousness. When he awakes, he finds himself in the sickbay back on the *Enterprise*, where the ship's doctor tells him 16 years have passed and he's now the ship's captain. Not only does Riker have no memory of the last 16 years, he's not aware that he's gotten married, his wife has died, and he has a teenage son. To add to his confusion and tension, the *Enterprise* is engaged in a vital peace mission with the Romulans that could lead to a treaty between the empire and the Federation.

Needless to say, Riker is full of questions but the answers he receives – that he is the victim of a rare virus that has damaged his memory, selectively removing the last 16 years of his life, and how he became a key figure in the peace negotiations – don't truly satisfy him. When Riker realizes his "son" can't really be his child because the woman who was supposedly his dead wife is actually just a reflection of an old holographic experience, his suspicions are confirmed. As he confronts his crew with questions they can't answer, the entire charade quickly collapses. Riker discovers he's trapped in a giant Romulan holodeck and that the fake *Enterprise* and his false son were merely illusions created to dupe him into revealing Federation defense secrets.

Riker's Romulan captors introduce him to a fellow prisoner: a young boy who they say was used as a template for the son Riker met in the holographic projection. As the two of them escape their captors and seek a hiding place, Riker soon realizes that this is yet another projection. He confronts the boy, who finally breaks down and tells Riker the truth. He is actually a young alien refugee who, trapped on this remote planet, lonely and isolated, used his people's advanced technology to kidnap Riker and create an alternate world for him. The alien boy's motivation is utterly human – he simply needs a father.

Each twist in the story was carefully set up to be fair to the audience with the requisite clues fixed in the proper places. The biggest clue is the alien boy – who first takes the guise of Riker's son, then as a prisoner of the Romulans, then finally in his true form as an abandoned child lost on a deserted planet. This intriguing and accessible character is present throughout the story and his mere existence, and the way the character is portrayed, is the biggest clue of all. Not unlike *The Sixth Sense*, the heart of the story is a relationship between a man and a boy who ultimately need each other. What could have been a derivative and unsatisfying spy plot about Romulans trying to dupe a Starfleet officer is transformed into a touching tale of a lonely child seeking love and family.

Comedy set-up/pay-off

Artful set-ups and pay-offs can enhance any genre, and it doesn't have to be with a twist ending. Two more recent examples are *Legally Blonde* and *My Cousin Vinny*. In both of these comedies, one character's superior knowledge about a subject is stated and restated, and passed off as an amusing character trait. In Dale Launer's *My Cousin Vinny* (1992), Marisa Tomei won an Oscar for her performance as the auto-expert, gum-chewing, street-smart girlfriend to the story's hero, Vinny. It is her character that rescues Vinny's legal case when he puts her on the stand, after they've had a bad argument and she's decided to walk out on him. In her rage she points out what an idiot Vinny, as well as the prosecution, must be to assume that the getaway car could have been the one in question, because the tires that left their mark at the scene of the crime couldn't fit that model and make of car. Vinny wins his case, and wins back his gal, demonstrating to her that he *does* know how helpful and intelligent she is.

In Karen Lutz and Meredith Lynn's *Legally Blonde* (2001), the protagonist is a gold-coiffed sorority girl with expertise in cosmetics, clothing and hairdos, who goes to her local salon regularly for solace and to render advice. While being perceived as mentally vacant at the law firm where she is interning, it is her knowledge of hairdos that trips up and exposes the lies of a fellow sorority girl on the witness stand, thereby winning the case and proving herself more than a dumb blond.

The Aristotle connection

Aristotle says that everything in a dramatic story must be there for a reason. Anything that is at all extraneous should be cut. Setup material is material that should otherwise be cut. It's woven into the early potions of a story, planted so that it may grow and blossom, and often hidden behind or utilized as characterization or business to cover dialogue sequences. The trick is making sure that the dialogue is interesting and important enough so that the audience doesn't concern itself with the fact that our character never finished fixing the banister or those damn brakes. If the proper work isn't done early in the story, the pay-off will not only be predictable but obvious and contrived. The set-up is there for a reason, but one that is not revealed until much later. Otherwise, a lead character's knowledge of cars in *My Cousin Vinny* or hairdos in *Legally Blonde* would have been extraneous. The fact that no one ever talked directly to the child shrink in *The Sixth Sense* would be an unnatural flaw. The fact that only those that go with Death can see him in *One for the Angels* would be an intriguing idea that didn't pay off.

Perhaps we, as an audience, appreciate set-ups and pay-offs so much because they relate to one of the great mysteries and pleasures of life. We never know how a connection will play out in our lives – what jobs we might get because of who we once met long ago, or how a certain piece of knowledge we learned and thought was totally useless suddenly became advantageous – or at least made us look smart. Or who we might meet as a result of meeting someone else. Isn't it true that we like to feel that we are all connected? Isn't everything all really truly connected in some way? Perhaps part of our enjoyment of set-ups and pay-offs is a desire to believe that things happen for a reason, that there is karma, that good things come to those who wait and that what goes around does come around.

Stories are a form of making a connection. What could be more fitting than making a tale that successfully illustrates the value of human connection with creative set-ups and pay-offs? So go forth and set up something and pay it off. Maybe your next screenplay will be the set-up that pays off big time.

What did we learn?

Whether the set-up takes the form of a *The Twilight Zone* style twist, a simple plot element, or a comic approach, always use an appropriate and satisfying pay-off that is fair to the audience.

The best set-ups and twists are built out of believable and accessible characters that provide a strong foundation for the plot.

Don't forget your Aristotle. Everything has a reason.

Exercise

Create two premises, working backwards. In the first, generate an astounding plot twist ending, the more over the top and off the wall the better; such as a story where a police detective turns out to be an alien, a woman hairdresser is exposed as a man, a murder mystery with a shocking reveal, a plot where two children learn their parents are not actually their parents. Just focus on the ending, as surprising and unexpected a climax you can think of, no matter how absurd or unrealistic it may feel to you. Now, working backwards, create a plot that leads to this revelatory climax. Plan the clues, build the structure, and make it work. Be prepared to get lost on the way; you may not be able to get to your amazing pay-off realistically or believably.

Now look at this same premise and ground it in character. Why does this particular character need to go through this specific story to achieve a meaningful change? You may have to start over and junk the entire structure of the piece but focus on the human being at the center of your story. This will be difficult but, if you do manage it, you just might have a truly interesting story on your hands.

Bonus exercise

Another simpler exercise is to create a comic or dramatic runner based on a single line or character quirk. If you have a completed project, or are about to start one, try to give your protagonist or a major supporting character a key line, bit of business, or character quirk in the final act of your film. Now work backward and establish it throughout the story. The rule of three should apply: use the runner at least three times.

11 Writing for a budget

When the Indian politician Kapil Sibal said, "We're trying to create a better world, not a perfect one. It cannot ever be perfect," he was referring to how to best govern the world's largest democracy. However, his words could be attached to any creative endeavor – an oil landscape, a narrative poem, a theatrical play, or a feature film's screenplay – which depends on a distinctive, accessible world to support its plot, character, and themes. Perfect is not possible in any aspect of human affairs, but the world is still what we make it, literally, when it comes to the environments that artists create in their works. The worlds can't be perfect; in fact, the more imperfect the more drama, conflict, and challenge available in the story being displayed or told. The balance between creating a well-defined and believable world whose imperfections can properly power the energy of its narrative and efficaciously building that environment within a project's particular budget is perhaps the key challenge of producing any such piece.

Whatever the size or scope of a project, the complexion of its world defines the nature of its story, theme, and characters. No matter the resources available for a particular film or its desired audience, intention or concept, a carefully constructed environment is crucial to a feature film's ultimate success. As with every element that matters in the final, edited product, it all begins with the screenplay. Its world will define its characters, plot and theme as much as these individual elements work on their own. But beyond any aesthetic or creative aspects, the feature film screenplay serves as a production blueprint for often elaborate and expensive entertainments designed to communicate through sound and image its engaging, intimate and/or emotional concepts to a mass audience, whether in the screening room of a multiplex or the living room of a home. This art form, usually so impersonal, commercial and crass, yet often extremely personal, thoughtful, and challenging, always depends on a solidly constructed world or environment no matter its basic intentions or audience.

Micro-budget feature

Creating a world that is designed for a limited budget or resources, yet is still successfully cinematic is particularly difficult. A tight budget is not necessarily a serious disadvantage in a project that uses an intentionally limited environment to enhance the drama and suspense of a story while still exploring large themes. In DC's career, he experienced these advantages co-writing (with Jack Rhodes) and co-producing a low-budget horror film, *Mr. Hell* (2006), which was set largely in one location, a warehouse in Houston, Texas, and shot on a restricted schedule of 21 days. The limited locations and cast kept the project's budget low enough to make it realizable while still providing a sense of claustrophobic and enclosed horror that was filmic and dramatic. *Mr. Hell* was successful, earning a wide release via DVD and Netflix.

On another project, *The Red Queen* (2008), which DC directed, co-wrote (with Jack R. Stanley) and crewed as a class project at the University of Texas Pan American, he took advantage of the university's facilities, locations, and resources to expedite production. He wrote to what he had – the campus and its offices, his department's theater and its scenic areas – using only what was available. The end result won several significant honors, including the Silver Palm Award at the Mexico International Film festival, and was distributed through Echelon Studios. A key reason this project succeeded as well as it did, despite a budget of under $15,000, was that DC had designed the story to take advantage of the resources that were available; a perfectly logical approach that often eludes low-budget or independent filmmakers.

Dark Tarot (2014) is another example of a micro-budget feature film (made with a student crew) written specially with the limitations in available resources in mind. Micro-budget horror film producer Geraldine (or "Ger") Winters of DGW Films had made several extremely low-budget and deliberately campy horror films that received limited foreign and internet distribution. Making these low-budget films was her passion and hobby and something she enjoyed doing even if she never made a profit from them. She understood that what she needed to do when writing her scripts was use very limited characters and a very confined location. Ger approached DL because she had access to a new, empty $3.5 million mansion in a secluded area of New Jersey and she wanted to use a student crew to shoot a micro-budget thriller within it. After a scout of the location, Ger and DL came up with a story that could be thoroughly told within the mansion, with a few minor extra scenes that could be shot at Ger's home and within a small studio at a college.

The result was the supernatural thriller *Dark Tarot*, a tale about four trophy wives who arrive at an empty mansion to bid on the diary of the dead young man they all had affairs with and whom one of them killed. The character list became four women in their 30s, one young female spirit medium, the ghost of the handsome dead pool boy and the older butler who turns out to be a blackmailer. Designed to be shot in 10–14 days, the screenplay was set almost entirely inside the mansion with only a few other locations to support its flashbacks, such as a swimming pool, dining room, the front gate of an expensive home, a mailbox, etc. All simple settings the producer already had access to, which drastically reduced the need for company moves. Writing a story set in an empty mansion also allowed less expense for art direction – although some props and furniture had to be brought in. These restrictions helped dictate the way in which the story would be told and visualized. The film was shot in 15 days and gained release on Amazon Prime.

A poorly supported environment has led to the creation of a variety of low-budget projects with thinly realized, unconvincing, even laughable worlds, as anyone who has seen Ed Woods' *Plan 9 from Outer Space* could attest. For more recent examples take a look – a very brief one – at any of the many low-budget zombie or found-footage films produced recently, including *Zombie Strippers, Gang of the Dead, Redneck Zombies, Area 407, Apartment 53, The Dead Inside,* or *The Devil's Due*. Even George Romero, the writer-director who arguably launched the American flesh-eating genre wave with *Night of the Living Dead* in 1968, failed to find satisfying creative meat in his own combination of the found-footage and zombie formats, *Diary of the Dead*. The production of these projects may make perfect sense financially; they can be shot on lean budgets and schedules in economic environments with small casts, offering a quick return on a relatively small investment. But if the stories are familiar, trite, and stale, or their characters thinly developed and clichéd, the film will literally not be worth watching let alone producing.

Paranormal Activity (2007), the first of the recent spate of low-budget found-footage films, contained the advantage of offering an exciting, innovative approach to a sub-genre that actually dates back to the execrable *Cannibal Holocaust* and the endless yawn that was the first *Blair Witch Project*. Shot with a tiny cast entirely in a single location – the producer's house – the characters, concept and visual approach of *Paranormal Activity* pulled the audience into a satisfying and unexpected experience. However, this particular well has been pumped dry by its many increasingly pale imitators, even within the *Paranormal Activity* "franchise" itself with its multiple sequels of diminishing quality. Some of these found-footage films, like *VHS* and *XX*, have used an omnibus format to produce a fresh take on the concept. But it would be advisable for writers to steer clear of a zombie, faux documentary, or limited-location horror project unless they possess a particularly fresh and intriguing idea that will carry them and their audience to an interesting, frightening place.

In any case, movies are made on a wide range of budgets. Most writers don't think about the budget when they write, but there has always been a market for quality low-budget scripts and, with the advances of digital video, there are even some companies that are only looking for screenplays that can be done on a shoestring. These films can often launch careers for actors, directors and writers.

But won't writing for a budget influence, potentially limit or impede a writer's creativity? Yes and no. A good example is Peter Hedges' screenplay for 2003's *Pieces of April*.

Independent low budget

Peter Hedges was an experienced and successful writer, but he wanted to direct. Getting the opportunity isn't easy for any first-time director so Hedges needed to write something that could be done on a low budget. He made sure that his story didn't demand any elaborate setups, special effects, animation, crowd scenes, car chase scenes, stunts, guns, gore or expansive photography. Character is what Hedges concentrated on and it is what carried the film, which was shot on Mini-DV yet received national theater distribution.

Hedges limited his locations to simple, easy-to-find places – a few cramped New York City tenement apartments, a thrift store, a family car and a few roadside stops such as gas stations, doughnut shops and a diner. Conversation, not visual action, drove the story through these locations. Most low-budget films are big on talk and low on action; generally lacking diversity both visually and emotionally. Hedges avoided this mistake by intercutting between the three simultaneous tracks of his story, thus adding action and variety. But, most of all, Hedges gives us a diverse selection of characters that keeps us engaged.

In *Pieces of April*, the titular April is the black sheep of the family, living in the burned-out East Village with tie-dyed hair and a boyfriend. She is trying to make a Thanksgiving dinner for her estranged family from the suburbs. Her mother is dying of cancer and they haven't seen each other for years. When April's oven doesn't work, her journey begins – to find a stove and her inner feelings.

Bobby, her boyfriend, leaves her during her quest to go off on his own. He has a "thing" he has to do. As Hedges sends Bobby on his own journey he sets up questions in our minds about what Bobby is doing. While the young man hangs out in a burned-out lot making calls to meet someone, we suspect the worse, only to discover that Bobby is meeting a friend who runs a thrift shop where he intends on getting a suit to impress April's folks. His journey is not one of criminal enterprise but of seeking acceptance.

The funniest, most emotionally complicated journey is the one April's parents and siblings go through, with Hedges exposing each character during their drive together towards New York. Whether it's the loving father who tries to hold things together, the bitter mother who resents dying and refuses to be nice, the forgetful but loving grandmother, the bossy younger sister and the quiet artistic brother, their mini odyssey is one of a family dealing with the inevitable.

Hedges offers us three-dimensional characters fighting for space in a cramped, confined location – the family car. Each is well rounded, if a mixed bag. While we dislike the sister who puts down April and tries to turn the family back, we feel for her when her mother insults her beautiful singing. The mother Joy is anything but her name. She is rude and spiteful to her mother, her daughter, and her husband, though gentle to her son. While we dislike her, we feel for her as she throws up at road stop after stop, dying a little more each mile. Hedges softens her meanness with a sense of humor, such as when she insists they bury a squirrel they hit on the road. This is a journey for her as well; perhaps her last.

The monotony of the inside of the car is broken up with Hedges switching between the family on the road, April in her neighbors' various apartments, and Bobby's shopping and eventual fight with April's old boyfriend – of which we only see the outcome. This is an excellent way to add visual activity and filmic imagery to a low-budget film without any Hollywood-style stunts or pyrotechnics. Hedges' greatest work is in his use of, or lack of, dialogue. It is often what is left unsaid that speaks the loudest about Hedges' characters and their situations. Much is inferred and revealed through a sparseness of speech rather than through extended talk, which not only works wonderfully for the story and the characters, but for the budget as well. The less dialogue, the fewer takes; the fewer takes, the faster the shooting; and the faster the shooting, the lower the budget.

This is an ensemble cast and an ensemble story. In total, it is no small cast, yet there are no crowd scenes until the very end. With the structure of Hedges' multiple journeys, shooting days with small casts are simple and mandatory. Scenes are kept simple, as this is a modest tale of complicated emotions. Nothing was sacrificed in the script for sake of a low budget since this was a story that didn't need a big budget. Hedges let the characters and their emotional journey carry the film, which should happen in any movie regardless of its production resources.

Hollywood low budget

We can see that the more daring approach to writing a low-budget script – daring in the sense that it's especially difficult to pull off – is to create a high-quality drama with a strong theme, strong characters, and strong plot. 2010's *Winter's Bone* – screenplay by Debra Granik & Anne Rosellini, based on the novel of the same name by Daniel Woodrell – is another superb example of a strong story written to take advantage of limited resources.

First of all, the script is short: only 72 pages. Considering the thin schedules within which most low-budget films are produced, it makes no sense to attempt to shoot a screenplay past 80 or 85 pages in length when you simply don't have the time or money to properly record them. For low-budget movies, less is more, which means fewer pages, locations, and cast. The amount of night shooting as opposed to day shooting must also be considered – it takes more time and money to light and shoot at night than during the day. Even the number of days within which a story takes place needs to be examined. Every day that a character experiences their fictional "life" in the story may necessitate a costume change and every piece of wardrobe, often tailored to each actor, costs money. It's also a given that scenes involving children, water, and animals should be avoided. Children require short hours, which can severely limit your shooting time in a day. Animals are often difficult to work with, which can cause costly retakes. And shooting on the water can be a nightmare; just ask Steven Spielberg who went 100% over budget and schedule on *Jaws*.

The killer factors in producing a film are period, locations, cast, and effects. For *Winter's Bone*, the cast is small, the visual effects non-existent, locations limited, and the period contemporary. Most of the action occurs in lead character Ree Dolly's house. Another house stood in for two additional locations – front and back. But, as can be seen in some of the titles previously mentioned, limiting your story's locations is not a magic potion that can always create the perfect low-budget film. While the Ozarks of Missouri where the film was set and shot was visually filmic, *Winter's Bone* truly shines in its story and casting. Great care was given to a plot and characters that served an intriguing premise – a mix of murder mystery, personal drama, and social commentary. The script is a lean, quick, read and, like all truly good stories, the characters carry the action, not special effects or stunts. A simple but important challenge – Ree trying to find her father, who has skipped his bail, to save the family home – pushes the plot forward through rising action, obstacles, and reverses; all those Aristotelian elements every good story should have. It's no wonder this movie launched Jennifer Lawrence's career and gained four Academy Award nominations, including one for its writers for Best Adapted Screenplay.

A final point must be made – *Winter's Bone* did employ children, animals, and scenes on water. Rules are made to be broken.

Limited-budget TV

Working sensibly and carefully with what you have doesn't apply to only feature film productions. It can be argued that a television show is a series of low-budget projects, each episode produced in a limited period of days with proscribed schedules and casts. Even a high-budget series like *The Walking Dead* will employ a "home" or standing location each season – such as the prison in seasons three and four and the Alexandria subdivision in later seasons – to provide permanent sets to facilitate production. In DC's own experience on shows like *Star Trek: The Next Generation* and *Diagnosis Murder*, he was grateful for the availability of the standing sets of the starship *Enterprise* and County General Hospital respectively. Without those sets these productions would have been forced to rebuild their world for every episode at a cost prohibitive for most television productions – a strong reason we no longer see many anthology series like *The Twilight Zone* or *Outer Limits* very often.

In any case, even for a television series, the standing sets or world should be as filmic as possible, which is why TV series tend to take place in interesting, dramatic, or cinematic locales like police stations, hospitals, spaceships, and apocalyptic worlds. Even series set in "ordinary" worlds tend to be high comedy or dramas like *The Big Bang Theory* or *This Is Us*. A well-defined and designed environment is crucial to any television or film project, especially when the resources are extremely limited.

What did we learn?

Know your budget.
Write to your budget.
Create a believable and filmic world, no matter your budget.

Exercise

The only difference between a guy selling newspapers and a producer is the producer has a screenplay under his arm. A producer is defined not by a fancy office on a studio lot but by the projects or properties they control. This is worthy of repetition: the real power of the producer is in the properties he or she controls. Therefore, when a writer finishes a screenplay, they are automatically a producer since they now control a property. A writer certainly does not need to produce every script he or she writes but, since a writer is a producer when they finish a script, then why not write a script they can produce?

One of the most successful producers of all time was Roger Corman, the man who gave us so-bad-they're-good classics like *Little Shop of Horrors, Comedy of Terrors*, and *Teenage Caveman*. Not only did he never pursue a project he did not have the immediate resources to produce, he would usually shoot a second film back to back with the first to re-use its props, crew, cast, and locations, thereby making two films for the budget of one and a half. While critics would sneer at the vast majority of movies that Corman produced, he often said he never lost money on any film he made, which is probably true.

As an exercise in approaching a project as a true writer-producer, think of all the distinctive props, costumes, locations, and production resources over which you have absolute control. You live in a house or apartment; those are potential locations. You have a doctor in the family that will loan you their scrubs; that's a costume. You have a cousin who drives a laundry truck, willing to let you borrow it for a weekend; that's a picture vehicle. Your grandfather has an old hot-dog cart; that's a prop. List anything that you know that is immediately available and is at all filmic, dramatic, colorful, or narratively useful. Then build a premise around those elements and take a long look at what you've ended up with. If this is something that intrigues or excites you, then proceed to write an extended premise or outline, if not a screenplay, that focuses on those elements. In this manner you will proceed like a Roger Corman-style writer-producer, working only with what you know you have.

This approach tends to work best with limited-location, contained projects. As an example, let's say you have a uniform your brother wore when he was working at a fast-food stand, your Dad's 1968 Chevy Nova, and your grandmother's farmhouse in the country. This could give you the basic production support for a horror film where the ghost of a fast-food worker is terrorizing a group of teenagers in an isolated location in his ghost car. Or let's say you or members of your family own or manage a flower shop, bar, restaurant, insurance office, chicken shack or car lot: any kind of business where the owners will allow you access late at night or on the weekends. You can now design a drama or comedy set in any of these locales. Whether or not you ever produce the premise or screenplay you create, you will arrive at a possible project that will be at least economically attractive to other potential producers.

Bottom line, the difference between a writer and producer is only a hyphen instead of a conjunction. Try it on. Writer-producer. How does that feel?

12 Rewriting
The pain and the gain

"The beautiful part of writing is that you don't have to get it right the first time, unlike, say, a brain surgeon." What Robert Cromier said about the writing of novels certainly applies to the writing of screenplays. It's a cliché even Robert Towne, the genius behind the script for one of the best-written movies of all time, *Chinatown*, is willing to repeat: "Every good screenwriter that I know of spends an awful lot of time rewriting." Good writing is rewriting. But how do you know when you're actually making the script better as opposed to making arbitrary changes for the sake of making changes: simply spinning your wheels? We've all known writers who can't let go of a project who endlessly scribble their way through every line and scene in a blind, pointless search for the "perfect" draft when (a) who defines what is perfect, and (b) there is no such thing as perfect. At least not in human affairs on this planet anyway. So how does one sensibly and productively approach improving a screenplay?

As in all creative issues involving any kind of writing, it's a matter of critical judgment and logic. Every element of a screenplay presents a series of decisions. Where does the story start? Who is the story about? Where will the story begin and end? Where does each scene begin and end? Let's assume you've found the answers to all of these key questions and worked your way through the bulk of the heavy lifting that is the creation of the complete first draft of a screenplay. If you want to launch a sensible revision process and make it better you'll have to re-examine all of your decisions. It may be as simple as changing the choice of words here and there: a polish of a particular piece of action, setting, or dialogue. We should all be fairly comfortable with that style of simple revision.

But how does a writer revisit the story elements and character beats, the plot points or key events, the money scenes and jaw droppers? We pull on one thread, we yank at this or that plot element, and the entire piece could start to unravel. Serious rewriting can lead to an intensive reconstruction of the carefully assembled edifice that is your screenplay, which may not always be the wisest course of action. If it isn't broke why fix it? Needless to say, the more logically and carefully you organize your first draft the easier your revision process should be.

To facilitate the best possible development of a solid first draft, a writer should always be aware that the first choice is almost always the worst choice. Every word, line, and idea should be carefully evaluated past that initial idea to avoid the familiar, the stale, and the predictable. Be careful with your dialogue. The sensible and usual ways people converse in certain situations will be trite and familiar on screen. If you have a character enter a post office to pick up an important letter, don't play it straight. Perhaps the character is nervous and sings to calm himself, or he makes inappropriate jokes with the clerk. Try to approach the moment from a fresh angle, any choice but the first.

Even as simple a choice as deciding on a protagonist's wardrobe and transportation should be given special care. Having a Texas character wear a Stetson and drive a Ford F150 might not offer the narrative possibilities of a trilby and an Edsel.

Usually revisions are required when the writer realizes late in the game that they've left something vital out – some crucial piece of information relating to the characters or their situation. Or the writer can see that a plot or character element has not been properly developed, or that some other piece of business has not been properly established. Backstory, the relevant history of the lead character or characters, is often where writers find themselves struggling because movies and TV shows are usually creatures of the immediate moment, the here and now. Backstory is often portrayed through flashbacks, voice-overs or montages that display the action that has occurred prior to the film's start. If these devices are not handled or placed properly, they can come off as clumsy or clichéd. How do you deal with the past in a screenplay when the present usually dominates its action?

There is something humorously referred to in dramatic writing as the dreaded "Dead Puppy Scene". It's the moment, usually added in a second or revised draft, where the character reveals their dramatic backstory. It's dreaded because often it comes out of left field and seems forced or out of place. An excellent, recent example of this kind of mistake can be found in the 2015 film *Spare Parts*, written by Elissa Matsueda, based on *La Vida Robot* by Joshua Davis.

In this otherwise entertaining movie focused on the true story of a group of high school Latino students who won first place in a college-level robotics competition, their teacher's backstory is not revealed until late in the second act. In a scene intended to be poignant, a friend of the teacher notices a picture of a little girl in his apartment. This drives the teacher to admit that the death of this daughter had a huge, negative impact on his life and career. The moment is clumsy and convenient, a chunk of backstory literally dropped into the script without any context or preparation to define and motivate a lead character far too late in the plot. This is not at all unusual; how many scenes like it have we seen in a hundred movies and TV shows? But it doesn't have to be. The best way to avoid the Dead Puppy Scene is by working in the backstory bit by bit.

Working in backstory

Screenwriter Andy Breckman is the creator, head writer and story editor of the USA TV series *Monk* (2002–2009). DL had gotten to know Andy over the years as an off-and-on acquaintance. He was generous enough to give him a copy of the first draft and the final draft of one episode to use in his screenwriting class as an example of rewriting and working in backstory.

"Mr. Monk Goes Back to School" (2003), written by Andy's brother David Breckman, was the season two premier. The story centers on a science teacher at a prep school that murders the female English teacher with whom he was having an affair. Of course, the killer has an iron-clad alibi at the time of the homicide; he was giving an exam when his girlfriend fell from the clock tower. We know he did it, and right away so does Monk. The question is how.

There are some major and minor differences between the first draft and the final fifth draft. In the first draft, Monk and his assistant Sherona are playing a very funny game of chess. If you haven't seen the show – and you should, it's well written – Monk has OCD, so he is constantly centering all the pieces in each square. When Sherona opens with her queen, Monk gets ready to take it. But Sherona licks it. Now he can't bear touching it and claims she's cheated while she claims he's been molesting all the pieces throughout the entire game. This scene expertly sets up their unique relationship and quickly demonstrates Monk's character flaws (a sprinkle of backstory). At this point, the game is interrupted by a phone call from the female principal of the prep school.

In the first draft, the principal comes to Monk's apartment. She remembers Monk and his deceased wife, Trudy, from when they attended the school. Monk agrees to look into the apparent suicide as a favor to the principal, who doesn't believe the female teacher would have killed herself. By the end of the scene, the principal notices the chess game and asks why Monk didn't take Sherona's queen. He responds, "I'm waiting for it to dry." A great setup and pay-off.

In the rewrite, Monk and Sherona go to the principal's office instead of her coming to see him. Now, the principal and Trudy were "like sisters" while attending this prep school. Many of DL's screenwriting students were disappointed in the change, as it lost the great punchline about the queen. But DL felt that Andy, as story editor, made the right call in asking for the change. First, two scenes following each other in the same location is visually boring. Second, and more important, having Monk and Sherona visit the principal's office gave Monk the opportunity to point out a picture of Trudy in an old school photo on the wall. While this is the photo-gives-us-information moment again, it works well here because the context has been so carefully established, including making the principal a schoolmate of Monk's dead wife, rather than an old teacher. This allows the principal the opportunity to reveal more memories about Trudy, which also helps reveal how much Monk misses her.

This is all backstory and subplot and not the main mystery plot but, since we writers tend to focus more on the central plot in our first drafts, it is the backstory and subplots that often need the most reworking in any additional drafts. In this episode of *Monk*, the central story in draft one and draft five barely changes at all. It is the subtle extras that change and make the story all the more interesting and charming – the working in of backstory.

In the first draft, Monk remembers the big oak tree that he and Trudy used to sit beneath. At the closer, Monk touches a carved "Monk & Trudy" in the tree's bark. In the rewrite, Monk never attended the school, but the principal reveals to him that Trudy would always sit under that tree and write poetry by herself – great poetry that no one read. When she asks Monk if he ever read any, he replies, "I read them every night." In the closer for the final draft, the principal is searching for Monk, to thank him. Sherona replies, "He's with her."

```
Monk is 30 feet away, standing near Trudy's oak tree. He's
holding a HIGH SCHOOL YEARBOOK. It's open to a photograph.

CLOSE-UP- YEARBOOK PAGE- PHOTO

B&W photo of a young TRUDY, age 16, reading under the oak tree.

RESUME

Monk reaches out and touches the tree. Touches his late wife.
```

This is so much more powerful than the cliché of carved names in tree bark. This is what working in backstory does, whether in TV or in films. It allows us as writers to reach out and touch something deeper – in our characters and in our audience – and perhaps in ourselves.

The development rewrite

The rewriting of a screenplay is part of the standard development process of making a movie. The original screenplay may be what was sold and what got the writer in the door. But the development route with input from others both financially and artistically invested in the project is where the hard work is done in getting a script ready for production.

Sometimes a story can take a severe right turn as was the case with 1990's *Pretty Woman*, written by John F. Lawton. The original draft was decidedly bleaker, with its streetwalker protagonist, Vivian, addicted to cocaine and abandoned on the street at story's end by the financier who hires her for the weekend. Even the title was darker. The script was originally called *3000*, which referred to the amount the financier paid Vivian for their one weekend together. This is the ending of that draft ...

EXT. BUS - DAY

An old Greyhound bus drives down the freeway from Los Angeles. It moves easily through the traffic. A small sign over the windshield reads: DISNEYLAND.

INT. BUS - DAY

Vivian and Kit are sitting in the bus. Kit is sitting next to the window, looking outside with a warm, happy smile. She is so excited she can barely stand it.

>   KIT
> Could I get one of those balloons?
> You know, with the ears?

Vivian sits next to Kit staring off with utterly blank and empty eyes. The side of her cheek is still bruised. She is wearing her mint green dress, but her hair is poorly done and lies limply around her pale face. Kit coughs.

>   KIT
> Oh, I guess that's stupid. Those are for kids.

Vivian blinks and glances over at Kit, tired.

>   VIVIAN
> No, babe. You can have a balloon.
> One with the ears.

Kit smiles happily and looks back out the window. Vivian stares emptily ahead.

FADE OUT

This is definitely not the sweet, feel-good, Cinderella-style ending of the final product.

Pretty Woman went through multiple drafts and multiple writers, eventually becoming much more audience-friendly with that much happier ending. However, despite all those drafts and writers, John F. Lawton is still the sole credited writer on *Pretty Woman*, and the film was a huge critical and commercial success. The story even treats the lead character of Vivian, despite the fairy-tale aspects of her story's conclusion, with ample doses of intelligence, compassion, and understanding. Would any writer be anything but pleased with this outcome?

Mark Norman wrote the first two drafts of *Shakespeare in Love* (1998) when it was being developed at Miramax. The script was shelved and then playwright Tom Stoppard, known for his play *Rosencrantz and Guildenstern Are*

Dead and as a bit of a Shakespearian scholar, was hired to rewrite the screenplay. Stoppard added a great number of Shakespearian references, removed some odd characters, enlarged and created others, removed the narration, changed the entire dialogue style and created a screenplay that won the Academy Award, a Writers Guild award, the New York Film Critics Circle award and won the film the Oscar for Best Picture, the British Academy Awards Best Picture, and the Golden Globe Award for Best Picture.

Producer Susan Aronson saw a backer's audition of DL's play *Deep Six Holiday*. The three-character, one-set dramatic piece had been produced professionally in several regional theaters and won a few theater awards and DL was trying to get some interest to get it to New York. Susan came as a friend to just lend some support and fill a seat, but after the reading Susan liked the story so much she optioned the play to be her next film project to take to Showtime for whom she had just produced a film that won an award at Sundance.

During this development process, the producer offered a series of notes on the ways she thought it could be improved. DL wrote a screenplay version of the play, trying to "open it up" by adding location scenes only referenced in the play. At one point, Susan gave a very standard producer note: the second act was dragging. She then gave a very interesting note: this is a movie, we need to see more people not just places.

That second note gave DL the idea of how to fix the first note as well. A character only briefly mentioned suddenly had an entire new scene, which breathed fresh life – and humor – into act two. But it also gave DL the idea to create more new scenes that weren't in the play. After the third draft Susan showed the script to a director, and he gave DL additional notes – can we divide this scene and move half of it away from the house, and how can we add more visuals?

Many of Susan's notes not only improved the screenplay, but DL went back to the original play and added in several of the new scenes. Bottom line, when we write our own "final" draft that we feel we are satisfied with, it doesn't mean it's actually final or finished. Dramatic works are fluid and can be changed and molded. This is especially true in the development stages. It is even done once the project is approved for production.

The production rewrite

Another challenge in screenwriting that can bedevil intermediate writers is the dreaded production rewrite. These are inevitable in almost all television series and films. There is never enough money, means or time to produce any project, no matter its ambition or budget, so compromises inevitably must be made. After the first draft is submitted, revisions are required to bring the project in line with whatever resources are available to shoot it. This is especially true when it comes to the number, quality, and scope of cast, locations, special effects, and stunts.

When DC co-wrote and co-produced a low-budget horror film, *Mr. Hell* (2006), the rewrites flew thick and fast throughout the shooting schedule as production progressed. Depending on the circumstance or situation, scenes had to be adjusted, revised, or cut. However, these revisions weren't always focused on a process of elimination. *Mr. Hell's* special effects crew was so adept and resourceful that a major scene involving explosions and fire was actually added to the film late in the schedule. Revisions can exploit new assets as well as remove liabilities. Bottom line, a writer in the midst of production has to think on their feet, killing their darlings or birthing new ones to take the best advantage of his project's available assets, all the while never losing sight of the story that's being told.

Above all, be flexible.

The process of revision in television can be even more frenzied than in low-budget filmmaking. As pre-, post- and actual production occur on a variety of episodes all at once, every conceivable issue can arise when it comes to locations, cast, schedule, and effects. However, there can be another production problem peculiar only to television – not enough script written to properly fill the running time of an episode.

One of DC's most successful and perhaps best-known efforts is "Future Imperfect" (1990), an episode of *Star Trek: The Next Generation* he wrote with J. Larry Carroll. In its story, Commander William T. Riker falls unconscious during an away team mission and awakens to learn that 16 years have passed, and not only is he now captain of the *Enterprise* but he has a 14-year-old son he doesn't remember. Set in an alternate universe, most of the episode takes place on the starship *Enterprise* with only a few scenes occurring in simple swing locations. The plot is relatively confined in its action, special effects, and world.

As the director Les Landau shot the episode, it became clear that the script was underwritten. Every day of production ended with the timing of the episode running short, requiring additional scenes to be created to fill in the lost space. These scenes could not add to the budget in any way; they had to be shot with the cast, props, and locations already established in the schedule. However, the scenes still had to move the story forward; they couldn't simply be filler. So, DC and his co-writer scripted pertinent moments set in corridors, turbo lifts, and the captain's quarters: whatever standing sets were currently available. However, by the next to last day of shooting, the episode was still 2 minutes short, requiring one more scene to be shot the next day, and the writers were completely out of usable ideas.

The writers met with the executive producer and producer and put their heads together, creating the idea of a scene which would focus on Riker coming to terms with being a father and accepting the son he doesn't know. In a moment set in a turbo lift, between Riker and his son, he admits he never felt he could be a father thanks to the poor relationship he had with his own, that he's sad he can't remember his son's first tooth, his first steps, or anything else about him, but that he wants to be a real dad after all. The boy then assures Riker that he has nothing to feel bad about, that's he's never let him down. Thrilled, Riker tells his son he wants to take him to the holodeck to run the Curtis Creek program so they can fish together.

Everyone involved in the discussion that led to the creation of this scene contributed important elements: the executive producer the lost childhood moments; Larry Carroll, a committed fisherman, Curtis Creek, and DC, who had recently lost his own father, the moment, true to his own life, where he told his dad he never let him down not long before the man died. True human experience informed the scene, which became the most important and dramatic moment in the episode, a moment that was, ironically, never originally intended to be written, let alone produced. In this case, a production problem led to a lucky accident that vastly improved the final product.

This also illuminates how, besides the usual challenges presented by the demands of format, production, and personality in crafting television, there is an actual artistic component as well. In the creation of "Future Imperfect", we can see how the process of creative collaboration and the personal intentions and perceptions of its producers and writers influenced the episode's most emotional scene, proving that, even in science-fiction television, there is art.

The post-production rewrite

Yes, even after the shooting is finished and the edit is made, there will often be times that the circumstances, audience expectations, or powers that be will require certain scenes to be rewritten. The most common among them is the ending. *Little Miss Sunshine* had three endings written. *Get Out* had two. The classic films *The Maltese Falcon* and *Laura* both had their endings changed after their studios' heads, Jack Warner and Darrell Zanuck respectively, screened the first cuts. Julius Epstein also rewrote several scenes for *The Big Sleep* almost a year after the film was finished but before it was given public release, and he never worked on the first script at all. All of these rewritten scenes definitely improved the finished films.

In any case, a writer should be prepared to revisit a project months or even a year or more after it was produced. Until a film is released or a television episode aired, literally anything can happen. Above all, be flexible.

A note on taking notes

Usually the most difficult aspect of working in a professional situation is taking notes in "the Room" – the production office, staff area, or writing space where the creative principals will meet to discuss a particular project. Working the Room isn't limited to pitching an idea, getting a job, or having lunch with your boss; it's also about a creative continuum that almost always involves clawing through many, many notes on draft after draft.

When it comes to this difficult process it must be addressed, first and foremost, that any writer worth his creative salt will be instinctively resistant to making any changes he hasn't decided on or initiated himself. Even in the case of an assignment where the characters, plot, or concept were not born with the writer, if that writer has any passion or feeling for their work at all, they'll still have a sense of ownership.

Second, the notes will sometimes be presented in an authoritarian, close-minded or dictatorial fashion, which almost anyone would find difficult to deal with. Finding a way to "interview" a difficult individual like this with politely offered questions is an art unto itself.

And third, even if the people involved are not difficult, their notes will often appear to be confusing, off the subject, or problematic. This can especially be the case on a television project. While the number of people in the Room on a feature project may be reasonable and workable – a director, a key star, and a producer or two – the Room for a television assignment may contain a dozen or more producers, staff writers, and production people, all giving plentiful and contradictory notes. Just keeping track of what is being said will often be even more grueling than making sense out of what is being demanded.

If the writer wants to remain with a project they must be able to take notes and revise their material sensibly in an efficient and productive manner while still maintaining a creative point of view or basic mastery of the project. However, if the writer simply ignores the notes that don't suit them or makes changes that don't really make sense, their time on the project won't be a lengthy one.

In dealing with notes, a writer must be aware that, no matter the situation, any particular draft of a script can stand improvement, and that the point of view of the people they're working with must have value (otherwise they wouldn't be in the Room in the first place.)

Three tricks to taking notes

First, you must react to absolutely nothing personally, even if the notes are addressed to you in a personal manner. Write them down, nod to indicate that you heard them and don't offer any defensive comments. Take the time to distance yourself from the note-taking process and then reread them and see if you still understand what was being offered and why. In these cases, time can be your friend. Time can allow you to become less defensive and reactive and give you a more objective point of view.

Second, if you get a series of notes from different sources, in or out of the Room, that all address the same issue, then that is a matter that must definitely be dealt with. Many people will give you potential ways to fix the problem, sometimes in a conflicting or confusing manner. You may hate these notes, they may even be inconsistent with what you were trying to write originally. But, beyond a doubt, if there is something fundamentally wrong with any particular moment in your script, you will have to fix it.

And third, your notes will often be dealing with a problem indirectly. There is something wrong somewhere else in the story, structure, or characters that the note is not properly focused on but is still trying to fix. The trick is for you to decipher what is the broken or damaged cog that's positioned in another part of your story that is generating your readers' negative reactions at this point in the script. Did you neglect to set something up? Did you set up something that you never paid off? Did you create a moment, character or idea in the script that directly contradicts another moment, character, or idea?

If you can master the mystery or challenge behind any given note in these situations, you'll be doing the work of a seasoned writer.

What did we learn?

Embrace rewriting. Change can be your best friend in a script.
Work in backstory as you rewrite.
Be prepared to rewrite for production.
Learn how to take notes without losing your mind or your temper.
And above all – and this relates to every word of every chapter in this book – be flexible.

Exercise

Write a scene between two people in a practical location where the characters are doing some kind of specific work – such as two detectives in a police station, two insurance agents in an office, two surgeons in an OR, two waiters in a restaurant, etc. Create a dramatic, emotional moment between these characters that doesn't lose track of the work they're doing. If they're child-service agents, they're arguing over a case; if they're lovers on a honeymoon, they're at odds over their future together; if they're dog catchers, the issue is the animal they're supposed to put down.

However you approach the scene, allow yourself as broad a canvas and as rich an environment as you can imagine, preferably in a particular town or city with a specific language and culture with which you're familiar. Set the scene in a specific season as well: winter, summer, fall, etc. Don't worry about backstory. Stay in the immediate present with these characters. Oh, and the scene can't be over three pages long.

Now rewrite this moment with the same action set in a much more confined location without losing any of the power of the scene.

Now rewrite it again, setting the action in an interior rather than an exterior location, or vice versa.

Now rewrite it with an additional element of backstory without making the scene longer than three pages.

Now change the sex of the characters. If they're both men, make them women. If they're a man and woman, reverse the sexes.

Now change the time period.
Now change the season.
Now change the city.
Now turn it into a comedy.
Get the idea?

13 Wrote the script, now what?

When you write a script on your own, your own original idea, without being paid, you have written a "spec script." It is called that because you have written the script on the speculation that you will sell it. The vast majority of movies are made from commissioned scripts, legally known as a "work for hire." That means the writer was hired by a producer to write the script, based on an idea the writer pitched to the producer or the producer's own idea or a book, short story, article, play, comic book, old TV show, old movie, etc. that the producer has bought the screen rights to. The ownership of these scripts belongs to the producer and or studio paying the writer and not the writer. The vast majority of writers earn their living doing work for hire. Less than 10% of all movies made are from spec scripts.

So why write one? Because that is how the vast majority of writers get in the door. If a producer likes your writing but not necessarily your screenplay, they may hire you to write a screenplay. Or if they like your screenplay, they may option it, which allows them the exclusive right for a period of time to shop your screenplay around to raise money to make it. Or a producer might buy your screenplay, in which case they now own the copyright to it and can change it or hire another writer to rewrite it without your consent. You'll have to let your baby go, but you will get your money and a screen credit.

Sometimes, producers like both your writing and your screenplay and in these cases they will retain you as the writer on the movie, but will ask for changes based on their thoughts and ideas, the director's thoughts and ideas, and sometimes even the star's thoughts and ideas. If you don't like the changes, you can argue your case and maybe even win. If you refuse to make any changes you're off the movie and they'll hire someone else to revise your material. If enough changes are made, your credit on your original script can be reduced from sole screenplay to co-screenplay, or even co-story by, depending on how much of your source material is left in the final product and/or how the Writers Guild of America (WGA) credit arbitration goes. So your goal is twofold. First, when you sell a screenplay, maintain your position as a writer on the project as long as you possibly can. Second, write (and rewrite) the best possible version of your script prior to showing it around. But before you give it to anyone in the business, please copyright it.

Copyright

This is easily achievable; simply access the US Copyright website at www.copyright.gov/help/faq/faq-register.html, pay the $35 fee per project and your material is copyrighted across the world throughout your lifetime as well as 70 years beyond your death.

No, you cannot mail your script to yourself and it will be protected. The only thing that proves is that you mailed a copy of this script to yourself on a particular date. It does not legally establish ownership or authorship. Registering your screenplay with the WGA also does not legally establish ownership or authorship. Only a certificated copyright legally does that.

Feedback

One of the first things any scribe needs is good feedback. We writers are almost always too close to our own material to be fair judges of what works and what might need improvement. Before we start to send out our screenplay or enter it in contests, we need to make sure that we have rewritten and reworked the script and story the best we possibly can. That means listening to the opinions and views of others and improving what we wrote. Getting friends and relatives to read our material is almost always useless; they have no experience in screenwriting, nor any expertise in the movie industry. So, how does one get productive feedback?

The most immediate method is to join a screenwriter's group where other writers can look at your work for what it is and what it is trying to be, rather than whether they simply "like it." Where to find a writer's group? Surf the internet. Most groups will meet only once a month, so don't be afraid of traveling to one. DL was in a group with a member who came as far away as another state. There are also virtual writers' groups you can join online. Do some research and you're certain to find a few options.

Writers' groups can also serve a dual purpose; helping you improve your social life as well as your work. When DC first moved to LA in the 1970s, he joined George Clayton Johnson's writing group. Mr. Johnson was not only an eminent and well-established artist brimming with knowledge, wisdom and experience (he wrote the first episode of *Star Trek* ever to air, several famous episodes of the original *The Twilight Zone*, and co-created *Logan's Run*), he also inspired such a supportive and nurturing environment in his group that DC formed several friendships that lasted for decades.

DL joined a writers' group in New Jersey, which provided not only quality feedback and inspiration, but also the incentive to keep submitting to contests, festivals and producers, which resulted in him winning a contest that got him an agent.

On the professional front, the Sundance Screenwriters Lab is a contest that awards a select few scribes the opportunity to come to the Sundance Ranch in Utah and work with a producer and/or director on rewriting their screenplays. There are a few other writers' retreats that offer something similar, but Sundance is world famous, established by the inimitable Robert Redford, and has extensive Hollywood contacts. In the past, both Disney and Warner Brothers TV have held contests where a small number of winning writers were hired by these studios to work with Hollywood writers on developing the scripts with which they entered the contest. In the past, these projects have been TV-series oriented.

This leads us to professional consultants or script advisors: people who will give you detailed coverage on your material for a fee. Please approach this matter carefully. Depending on the fee demanded or the source providing the service, this process can be extremely helpful or a total waste of money. YOU need to do a little background research on exactly who these people are that are charging you money to give you advice. They most likely won't be successful working writers; those people are busy writing for paid situations and don't have the time. So who are they?

They might be script readers, people employed by studios and production companies to read and do "coverage" on submitted screenplays (coverage being detailed breakdowns on the plot, premise, and creative and commercial value of said screenplays). Depending on how long they've been in the industry, they may or may not know anything. One of these folks, Jennifer Lerch, wrote an excellent book aptly titled *500 Ways to Beat the Hollywood Script Reader*, which we highly recommend. Ms. Lerch has been in the biz long enough to recognize what helps get any particular script bought or passed on and how to generate material that will get the highest level of coverage.

But be aware that there is a difference between coverage and notes. Coverage is what readers do to summarize a script for the higher-ups who don't have the time (or desire) to read all the scripts that get sent in by agents, writers, actors, directors, relatives, friends of relatives, the limo driver, etc. Coverage is a synopsis of the story, what market it might appeal to, what films it's similar to, which actors might be right for it and whether the reader recommends it for this particular production company. If they do, it gets sent up to the ladder to the company's dreaded development executive, and, if they like it, they bring it to a production or development meeting.

Notes are comments on what works or what doesn't and there may be recommendations on possible script changes. Notes are best when they come from agents, development executives, producers, writers who have actually sold things, or directors who have actually shot films or television series in the industry. There are talented working professionals that have dry spells and offer these services to earn some spending money, and there are also talented successful people who just want to give back to those that are struggling. But be aware that these are few and far between. So before paying anyone for notes and coverage, make sure they have some experience and credits to back up their claims of being knowledgeable and helpful.

In the industry, the writer who has successfully gained the right level of access will inevitably be dealing with a producer who is reading their drafts and giving them feedback. Producers provide an audience and marketing view along with their own artistic ideas based on what they have worked on in the past and what they feel works. A good producer is a writer's creative best friend. Of course there are certain bad producers out there who want changes based on who they plan to cast, which market they intend to sell to, which director they like, what movie just made a ton of money, or what some drinking pal told them in a bar over scotch and sodas the night before. But the good news is that the vast majority of producers, both low and high budget, are truly committed to making the best movie possible. Their name will be on it, too. So, how does one find a producer? There are a variety of ways, which we will get to shortly.

There are also screenwriting contests that offer feedback on your script as part of the perks to get you to enter. Which brings us to …

Contests

There is an ever growing number of screenwriting contests that all charge submission fees to writers. Many of them are just moneymakers for the people running the contests, often with bizarre names or based in odd places. Contests come and go, but the longest-lasting well-respected ones include the Nicholl Fellowships, Austin Film Festival, Page and Scriptapaloosa. You can find lists of screenplay contests online but, at the writing of this book, the most notable websites are Moviebytes.com, FilmFreeway.com and Withoutabox.com. Moviebytes rates the contests while also offering writers a way to rate their own value of these contests. All these venues charge submission fees, which can definitely add up. Pick your competitions and budget your fees carefully. Depending on the quality of the contests you enter, or the quality of your work, this can be the best move an emerging scribe can make. Winning a major contest, or at least being one of the top ten finalists, can jump-start a writer's career.

Outside of title page and length requirements, most competitions have few limitations on their entries or the writers of those entries. No professionals need apply. In fact, the less working experience or credits a writer has, the more contests he or she will be allowed to enter. This includes some very significant and respected examples, like the Page and Nicholl Fellowships. For those events seeking emerging writers, any salaried experience and credits are actually a detriment.

There is almost no example of your work that cannot be entered in some contest somewhere, whether it's a feature, short, speculative TV pilot, or a spec episode of an existing series. Every conceivable genre – comedy, drama, thriller, family, faith or science fiction, western or historical, fantasy or horror, even musicals – can be placed in a rich variety of venues. There are certain advantages to writing a carefully researched historical project or a cutting-edge drama (whatever that might be these days) but any writer's project has a decent chance somewhere in this world if their work is at all up to snuff.

A few film festivals have screenwriting competitions and workshops as part of their schedules; the Austin Film Festival, or AFF, being one of the most noteworthy. DL had a friend from his writers' group who was a finalist in the AFF screenplay contest. While Nick, the writer, was in Austin, a producer who was a judge approached him and asked him if he would be interested in working on a screenplay. He smartly said yes and was hired very soon after to write a screenplay for the producer's film company. Serious and effective connections can be made at film festivals, if you are good at networking and socializing that is.

What you win through a contest depends on the contest. Some award a small amount of money, others writing software, many offer only a plaque or certificate, or even just a digital laurel sent to the winner over the internet. The important thing about screenwriting contests is who the judges are. The most respectable competitions have people from the industry reading the finalists' scripts. Actors are of no value as judges because they don't really have any clout as to getting a script bought. The truly valuable judges are junior agents, managers, producer assistants, and development executives: people in the industry who can recommend a script up the ladder to a producer. It's worth repeating that many a scribe whose work was within the top ten of a major festival found work as a writer.

However, the truth about these contests is that it is highly unlikely that the winner's script will ever actually get produced. Susannah Grant won the Nicholl Fellowship, and, even though her film was never made, she was hired as a writer on *Erin Brockovich* and went on to win an Academy Award. Now she's a well-established screenwriter who has directed a feature film.

Producers and agents

How do you get your script to a producer or agent? There are a variety of ways. One is by being a finalist in a script competition that has industry judges. Another is to send these people query letters. Never shoot a script to a producer, agent or anyone unsolicited: which means without their asking for it. This is considered unprofessional and turns people away. Instead you send them query letters within which you pitch your screenplay and yourself as a writer, hoping they will ask to read your material.

How do you find the development people and producers to whom you will send your query letters? There are a variety of sources, the primary ones being IMDB Pro and the Fade In *Online Writer's Guide to Hollywood Producers* (www.fadeinonline.com/product/writers-guide-hollywood-producers) as well as the old standard *The Hollywood Creative Directory*. YOU need to do your homework and only send your script to a company that makes films like the one you wrote. When you don't, they can get very persnickety, such as when a writer submits a feel-good comedy to Dimension Films – which only does horror – or a comedy to a company that only produces sports films (DL's manager did just that, even sending him in for a meeting with such an outfit. Nothing happened except for an intense discussion about New Jersey and Philly Cheese steaks – as the development guy was originally from New Jersey).

There are services that will write query letters for you. And there is the Virtual Pitch Fest that, for a charge per letter sent, will shoot your query letter/pitch to the development executives of companies that you pick – from a list of hundreds – via email. There is also Inktip.com, which, if you subscribe, sends you a weekly newsletter listing producers (usually low budget) seeking scripts and has a website where you can post a pitch and all the support materials – synopsis, script, and resumé – of your project.

If someone is interested in reading your screenplay, they will most likely offer you a standard release form to sign. This is a legal document that states that if the company produces a project with a premise or story similar to your screenplay you cannot sue them. Sign it. Young writers make the mistake of thinking someone will steal their idea. The truth is your idea may be new and original to you, but others may well have similar ideas they've already pitched or sold. Also, the vast, *vast* majority of film companies will never bother stealing anyone's idea, since they can easily pay a fee to just buy your idea that is very little for them but very nice for you. (The truth is the only people who ever seem to actually steal writer's ideas are other writers. For this reason some scribes prefer to not post their screenplays, or even their script pitches, online.)

There is a well-known independent associate producer who does nothing but pitch other people's ideas to studios and who takes a cut of the pitch purchase price. There are books and websites galore about how to sell your idea, or your story, or your script to Hollywood. Many of these are just moneymaking schemes, so be cautious and do background research on them before ever paying anything.

A final, limited mention must be made of agents. Yes, they do occasionally get writers jobs. Yes, there is a list of licensed agents available through the Writers Guild and, if you really want one, you can start there. Yes, you can contact them via query letters just like you would producers. Yes, once you are established you will need an agent to help you build your career and properly negotiate your deals.

However, for beginning writers, it's probably not worth the time and effort to pursue agency representation, at least until you have something serious – a purchase or staff offer, a major award win or a production deal – already in place to gain their immediate interest. Agents are usually too busy representing established writers to take on newbies, let alone respond to their queries, read their material, or meet with them. Agents will send scripts from multiple writers to the same producer – they want to sell a script and earn their 15% commission after all. Of course they want to sell your script, but they are just as happy if the producer buys another script from one of their other clients.

There are agents, managers (who take anywhere from 15–20% of your income), and lawyers. Any one of these can submit a script to a production company and negotiate a deal for you. Many emerging writers find lawyers to submit their work for them, with the promise that they will retain that lawyer to negotiate and write the contract if the script is bought.

A major word of warning – agents and managers NEVER charge their clients for anything. They do not charge for copies or postage, etc. They receive their money *after* the sale. There are unprofessional people out there claiming to be agents or managers that will tell a writer how great their script is and how they can sell it for a large sum of money, and then ask the writer for hundreds or even thousands of dollars in expenses. These are con-artists. Never pay anything, not even a "reader's fee."

They call it Hollywood

The premier headquarters of the film and television business is often misnamed Hollywood (where there are only two major studios physically located, but we digress). While numerous production companies may be headquartered on the East Coast, mainly in New York, the heart of the business is still situated on the West Coast in the sprawling city of Los Angeles.

Thanks to incentives and lower crew costs becoming widely available elsewhere, the major studios and production companies don't actually shoot the majority of their film and television projects in LA any longer. But while the physical manufacture of these productions may have emigrated all over the world from Atlanta and Vancouver or to Louisiana and New Mexico, the fundamental work performed in all key phases of pre-production – their writing, creative development, star casting, etc. – has largely remained in LA. Even though these television and film projects may be shot anywhere on the planet, they're almost always written not far from the beaches bordering the Pacific Ocean. The producers and development executives are quick to move their casts and crews to Bulgaria, but their hearts and souls still dwell in Beverly Hills.

When it comes to beginning or building a screenwriting career, it's a face-to-face business, and the faces that can buy your material or hire you for an assignment are almost always in Los Angeles. This means your face needs to be in that city and available for meetings, pitches, story conferences, and all the other conceivable phases of the marketing and development of your material. Even if you strike gold through a competition, an independent local production, or a singular connection through your cousin's brother's wife of Michael Bay's agent, for a screenwriter to nurture a career of any real duration your home will, by necessity, become Los Angeles, or at least New York or London or some other major production center.

If you're young, or not far removed from college, or an unattached "Sink" – single income, no kids – then heading out to Hollywood can be a reasonable and sensible option. Drive, fly or bus to LA, get a day job and a decent roommate, and jump into the deep end of the shark pool. Pretend you're enrolled in an extremely informal grad school for the uninitiated who want to become the initiated. Give it your best shot until you either succeed or reach that point where you realize you've simply run out of creative, emotional, or financial ammunition. If it doesn't work out, you'll always have a home to drive, fly or bus back to, wherever that might be.

If you do choose this option, then you must be prepared to pitch yourself and your material.

Pitching

It's not impossible to place a project without a direct, personal contact. DC sold an original screenplay, *Deep Dark Blue*, through the Inktip website to producers in the Netherlands without ever meeting with anyone in the process. However, this is the exception rather than the rule, especially if a writer wants to build and maintain a career of any length or quality. Again, it's a face-to-face business, which means your face needs to be physically in a room in Hollywood selling your ideas and yourself.

First rule: don't let them see you sweat. You may enter a situation feeling your entire career and your very life are on the line, but you can't expose that to your potential buyer, boss, agent, manager, whoever it is you're meeting with.

Second rule: if your potential buyer dislikes your idea or is even cruelly dismissive of it, do not take it personally, do not get pissed off, and do not leave in a huff. If they're willing to keep listening, then keep your head and keep pitching. On one occasion on a television series, DC kept pitching to the show's producers through rejection after rough rejection, until he actually reached his tenth story idea – which is when he got a sale that led to a script deal, and then to a staff position. Never give up, never surrender, and did we mention never let them see you sweat?

Third rule: have more than one script or idea to pitch. If they like you and/or your writing, but don't like the story you pitched, they will ask for "What else?" You need to have something else that you can submit to them ready to go. DC met a writer at George Clayton Johnson's writing group when he first joined it in the 1970s. This individual had finished a screenplay he was proud to show the group. It had a colorful, embossed, bound cover (which is an amateur move by the way). Ten years later, DC bumped into this writer at a science-fiction convention. Not only was the poor man showing around the same screenplay, it was the same copy in the same embossed cover, now worn and ratty.

You must have a basket full of eggs. Never head into a production company or the Room of a TV series with just one screenplay or one or two ideas. When the producer shoots down your first shot and asks "What else do you have?" be prepared to keep pitching through at least five more scripts or ideas. Don't forget DC and his pitch on that TV series; he got to the tenth premise before he got a sale.

Fourth rule: don't flog a dead or even a living horse. Keep your pitch short and sweet, under 3 or 4 minutes; maybe a little longer if you sense excitement in the room. Don't get lost in unimportant plot details, casting ideas, or thematic exploration. Reach the red meat of your story and bite into it quick. Please assume that, whoever you're meeting with, their time is valuable. Don't waste it.

Fifth rule: know what kind of projects the company you are pitching to made in the past. DL committed the big oops of pitching a historic pirate script to the development executive at the company that had lost millions on the film *Pirates*. That ended the meeting rather quickly.

Final rule: please don't depend on selling anything. Making productive contacts or connections can be much more important than booking a project. Pitching is a great way to meet and impress potential employers, if you handle it right. DC pitched to a producer on the *Bret Maverick* television series in the early 1980s and impressed the man well enough that, while that pitch did not lead to a sale, the same producer did hire him for *Walker, Texas Ranger* 13 years later. In the film business, you literally live and die off your contacts and connections; those faces in Hollywood.

How hard is pitching?

Pitching is a difficult process that can result in a truly epic level of frustration and pain. On one occasion, DC's agent told him a development executive at a production company based on the Warner Brothers lot was looking for action projects like *The Terminator* and *Road Warrior*. So DC went to the man's office with his then-writing partner and pitched a variety of notions along those lines. The development executive was not receptive, saying his company wasn't looking for science-fiction stories. A confused DC asked him what part of *The Terminator* and *Road Warrior* was *not* the science fiction he wished to pursue. The development executive just shrugged; he didn't know. He admitted he hadn't seen *The Terminator* or *Road Warrior*, he was just parroting something his boss had told him.

DC was so furious his writing partner had to walk him around the Midwestern Street on the Warner Brothers backlot, where they shot *The Music Man*, to calm him down.

Goodbye Hollywood

But what if you don't want to pitch? What if you have no desire to be face to face with any of those people in Hollywood? You truly like your hometown, wherever it is, and have scant desire to relocate to the land of packed freeways, smoggy skies and the occasional earthquake? What if you're older and wiser than some young college grad or Sink and you have a decent job, an established career, a business or a family: simply too much to lose? You don't want to upend your life, gamble with your future and swim with the sharks, but you still want to succeed, to achieve, to write that screenplay or television project. You want to see your work purchased, produced, distributed and lauded. What do you do then?

This brings us to …

Make it yourself

An abbreviated generation ago, when any production of any significance was shot on film, with the encumbrances of 35 or 16 mm cameras, the spools of footage contained within them, and the post-production of said footage, any independent filmmaker's options were limited. Thanks simply to celluloid, the cost involved in shooting any project of any length or significance was truly daunting. Even a feature limited to a single location and a cast of one would still require a budget in the tens, if not hundreds of thousands of dollars simply to illuminate, record, develop, and edit 80 or more minutes' worth of story.

In today's world, a mid-range HD camera, some Walmart fluorescent lights, a few terabytes of memory, a Mac with the full array of Adobe software, and some warm, determined human bodies can successfully produce the same 80 minutes in identical circumstances for a fraction of the cost – *if* whoever's in charge knows what they're doing.

That last part is the most difficult and demanding challenge. How does an amateur learn to create, work and produce at the level of a professional when they're teamed with other amateurs? There are natural talents, the occasional Steven Spielberg, Wes Anderson, or Robert Rodriguez, capable of genius almost from the start gun; but are you one of them? Most of us, including the authors of this book, had to learn their way through the business, being apprenticed with people more experienced than them, and being educated by professionals who were educated by the generation of professionals who were in place before them. Very few creative specialists learn, grow, and attain a level of marketable expertise when they're only training themselves, or working with individuals at their own level. This is the way of the world in every profession, whether it's screenwriting or skywriting.

It is conceivable that, through sheer dint of effort, hopefully by writing and producing a multitude of diverse personal projects, you could carry yourself in this field to wherever it is you want to go. Jim Jarmusch and his films come to mind on that score. Remember, the only significant difference between a producer and a guy selling newspapers is a producer has a script under his arm and not a newspaper. As soon as you finish a screenplay you are in control of a property and all that defines a producer is that level of control. However, though you may be able to write what you produce, will it really be worth producing? Will you have the inherent talent, expertise and/or resources to produce it properly?

If you are honest with yourself, and if the answers to these questions are a firm no, then where does that leave you? If relocating to Hollywood or doing it yourself is not appealing, practical or achievable, then where can you go?

This brings us to ...

Low-budget independents

Where do you find low-budget "indie" or independent film companies ("independent" meaning they have no studio or distribution connections, probably raised the money from their relatives or rich wannabe actors/directors, and, if they ever have profits, they're hiding them from the IRS) that are looking for scripts? We already mentioned Inktip.com, but there are other websites devoted to people who wish to make their own low-budget movies, like Stage 32 and Bluecat. These sites can offer webinars on everything from crowd funding to finding distributors. They can also provide additional services, such as script consulting, coverage services, and even online pitching opportunities. These are legitimate options, but, again, please proceed with the right level of research, caution and common sense.

Since they are usually working outside the mainstream studio system, indie companies can be more open to fresh material and more flexible at working with or hiring emerging writers. However, three key issues with independents must be mentioned. If you're working outside a Writers Guild contract or the Guild's protections, it may be difficult for you to get paid decently, on time(or at all), to protect your credit, and to get your back-end profits or fees if the film ever gets released (and many indie projects never see the light of day.)

How and how much?

Let's say your efforts have succeeded, whether it's through a contest, an indie, a website, or a singular connection through your cousin's brother's wife of Michael Bay's agent, and you've gotten an offer. You've actually secured the interest of a potential buyer in your original screenplay. You want to get paid, right? How does that work?

Show me the money – in the movies

As mentioned earlier, there are two basic ways for a producer to secure an author's original feature screenplay – an outright sale or an option. An outright sale is what it sounds like: the producer simply buys the script from you. An option is an exclusive "lease" on the screenplay for a specified period of time, usually from 6 to 18 months. During this time, whoever optioned the property can show it to producers, networks, or financial entities in order to secure funding, talent attachments, distribution, and/or a production deal. An option can be the first step to getting your screenplay produced.

It's not unheard of for a writer to agree to a free option on a work, especially when the writer is just starting out. If the company or individual offering such an option is well placed, authoritative or significant, then this is at least worth considering. However, it's the authors' experience that a free option is usually worth what the writer has been paid – nothing. If the company doesn't have a serious financial investment in your project, then their efforts to get it produced or funded will usually lack sufficient drive or intention to obtain said funding.

The authors advise all first-time scripters to secure at least the minimums for options and purchase agreements for their work as delineated on the Writers Guild of America website, whether they're Guild members or not. For example, if a producer can't provide a writer with 10% of the purchase fee for the option of a low-budget screenplay, which is currently about $6,000, then they're most likely not a legitimate buyer.

There are a rich variety of contracts and approaches available in selling or optioning a screenplay, or being hired to write one, all of which are laid out on the WGA website's current Schedule of Minimums at www.wga.org/uploadedFiles/contracts/min2017.pdf. However, there is one thing every writer should consider for every contract, whether it be low or high budget. With a reasonable ceiling on the film's projected production budget, let's say somewhere between $2 million and $5 million, you should always request your script fees be matched against 2.5% of the final budget.

This way, if you sell a screenplay that is originally intended to be a low-budget indie, and it somehow gets transformed into a high-budget studio production, you won't be left out in the cold with your initial minimums.

Show me the money – in television

In some ways, getting paid in television is much simpler and less challenging. There is rarely any negotiation on the basic script fees; the WGA minimums almost always pertain. Very few writers in this medium are hired through a freelance assignment any longer; most go to work directly on staff. Please take note of all those producers you see listed in the credits at the beginning of your favorite television series. Whether they're executive producers, co-executive producers, supervising producers, consulting producers, co-producers, or simply plain old producers, they all serve their shows basically as writers. This is why the many series being generated for today's Golden Age of television are often much better written than today's movies. Writer-producers are in charge of television; it's the directors and stars who are running the movies. Enough said on that score.

As is noted elsewhere, almost every script written for every TV series is conceived, written, and rewritten in the Room, which, considering the amount of money involved, the demanding production schedules, and the careers at stake can be a very stressful place. You gain access to the Room through your previous credits and reputation; your connections with the people already seated there; the speculative scripts you've written; or your agent or manager. The spec script can be an original screenplay, a script for the show itself, or a script for any high-end, state-of-the art TV series. This is where the script competitions can be helpful; a major win for an outstanding piece of work might actually get you into that Room.

A series contract for a new staff member can be a short one: anywhere from the first six to 13 episodes produced in the run of the full season of a broadcast show, which could consist of anywhere from 13 to 24 episodes. These contracts can be even shorter for the runs of ten or fewer episodes for a cable series. The object is to get your option continually picked up from season to season. To be a congenial yet productive member of the staff who doesn't disappear into the woodwork, yet still has enough creative presence to produce results without being strident or annoying, is no mean feat. Did we mention the Room could be a stressful place?

If you do find a seat in the Room, please take a piece of advice learned off the authors' bitter experience. Whatever the situation, whether the show is high or low budget, broadcast or basic cable, network or premium, make sure your agent includes as part of your contract a guarantee of at least one full script assignment beyond your staff fees. While a producer credit on a series is a fine and beautiful thing to obtain, your career will ultimately live or die on your script credits.

Don't undo your sale

One of the biggest problems young writers face when they actually, suddenly, have the opportunity to make their first screenplay sale are the naive conditions they suddenly attach, which almost always sink the project and cancel the sale. If someone wants to buy your first screenplay, don't insist on being the director, star or cinematographer as well. Just sell the script, take the money and the screen credit, and launch your career. With luck they will retain you as the writer on rewrites. If the movie ever gets made or even released (many films never get released even after they get made), you will be in more demand and able to demand more in future contract negotiations. Even just selling a screenplay allows you to get an agent, which allows that agent to sell you as someone who is hot and new and a superb talent everyone wants (whether it's true or not – because that's what agents do).

What did we learn?

There are basically five roads via which a new writer can travel to one of five worlds where they can achieve a successful screenwriting career.

One leads to the world of Hollywood. Move to Los Angeles and swim with the sharks as long as you can keep your head above the water.

The second road leads to the world of script competitions. Enter your material in the right places for the best results. So long as you believe in your material and in yourself, keep entering.

- The third leads to a world of websites that offer coverage, producer uploads, and pitching services. Buyer beware.
- The fourth leads you to the planet of do-it-yourself, which is hard to do if you don't know what you're doing.
- The fifth leads to the indie world, where almost anything can happen – including even getting your movie made. But will you get paid, will your credit be protected, and will your film ever be released?
- Pitching is hard, pitching can be frustrating, pitching needs to be short and sweet, and please don't expect to sell anything. You really pitch to make contacts.
- When optioning or selling a screenplay, make your buyer show you the money. Free options are usually not a good idea.
- Always copyright your material.
- Don't live or die on one project or idea; fill your creative basket with lots of eggs.
- On a feature-script deal, don't forget to contract a purchase fee that's guaranteed against 2.5% of your movie's budget, whatever it is.
- If you make a sale, take your money and run. Don't make unreasonable demands and kill the deal.
- Even if you're not a Writers Guild member, insist on being paid a fee that matches the WGA minimums listed on their website, whether your movie is low or high budget.
- If you get hired on staff, no matter the situation or your position on that staff, demand a guarantee of at least one full script assignment. Do not allow this assignment to be charged against your staff fees. If they really want you on staff, they'll want you to write that script.
- And whatever you do, whoever you are dealing with – especially in regard to any contests, websites, services, and producers – do your research.

Exercise

This is a long-term exercise, one not designed for the faint-hearted. In the course of 1 year or season, take your best piece of work and enter it in five significant or well-regarded contests. If you earn no recognition for that script, then put it aside, write another script and enter that in the same five contests. As the second script goes through its rounds, rewrite the first. If the second doesn't win anything, start entering the first again. And depending on what happens with those two scripts, write a third. And so on.

If you're serious about your work, you will continue with this approach until you have eventually produced at least four or five projects – hopefully of diverse subjects, genres, and approaches – at various stages of development that you'll be sending out to various competitions. If you have any talent at all, any ability to improve, any true desire to grow and achieve in this challenging field, something is bound to happen. Whichever of the five worlds described in this chapter, whichever road you decide to take, this exercise will be applicable.

Bottom line – writers write. They write whether someone pays them or not, awards them or not, likes their work or not. They write because they simply need to write.

If you're not that kind of person, if you don't possess that level of commitment – then why did you even bother to buy this book?

Index

A Beautiful Mind 13–15
A Fish Called Wanda 83–84
About a Boy 64, 68
Adaptation 66, 69
Agro 98–99
Aliens 59
American Beauty 51–52, 68
American Graffiti 21–23, 78
Aristotle 24, 29, 116
Arrival 37
As Good As It Gets 35, 64

Babel 80–81
Big Fish 16, 52–54
Big Sleep, the 35–37
Big Trouble 82
Billions (TV) 87, 92–95
Birdcage, The 61–62, 78
Blair Witch Project, The 71
Breaking Bad (TV) 3, 32–34

Casablanca 39–41
Catch Me If You Can 23–24, 99–101
Chicago 12–13
Chronicle 72–73
Citizen Kane 11
Cloverfield 71
Crazy Rich Asians 2
Crown, The (TV) 39

Dark Tarot 120
Darkest Hour, The 104–105
Deadpool 51
Diagnosis Murder (TV) 34, 92
Doctor Who 108–109
Don't Breathe 59
Double Indemnity 69–71
Dunkirk 80

End of Watch 73
Eternal Sunshine of the Spotless Mind 80

Fargo 7–8, 83
Ferris Bueller's Day Off 67
Fight Club 68

Game of Thrones (TV) 50–51
Get Out 113–114
Gone Girl 114–115
Gosford Park 84–85
Great Wall, the 3
Green Mile, The 78

Hard Way, The 7
Help, The 37
Hidden Figures 102–103

I, Tonya 101–102

Jane the Virgin (TV) 3–4

La La Land 3
Lady in the Lake, The 71
Last Broadcast, The 71
Lazarus Man 34, 92
Legally Blonde 116
Lincoln 37

Malcolm in the Middle 67
Memento 68
Miss Congeniality 6–7, 25–27
Modern Family (TV) 76, 87
Monk (TV) 128–129
Mr. Hell 120, 131–132
My Cousin Vinny 116

No Country for Old Men 57

Office, The (TV) 74–76, 87

Paranormal Activity 71, 121
Peaky Blinders (TV) 28–29
Pieces of April 121–123
Pirates of the Caribbean 6, 16, 18–21, 54–55, 57–58
Pretty Woman 129–130

Raising Arizona 67
Rambo 57
Red Queen, The 120
Red Violin, The 78
Revenant, The 106

Seabiscuit 97–98
Shakespeare in Love 106–108, 130
Shaun of the Dead 4–5
Sixth Sense, The 112
Spare Parts 127
Stand by Me 67
Star Trek (TV) 35
Star Trek: The Next Generation (TV) 34, 92, 115–116, 132–133

Starsky & Hutch (TV) 15
State and Main 81
Sunset Boulevard 41, 66, 69

Terminal, The 11, 59
This Is Us (TV) 87–91
Three Burials of Melquideas Estrada 60
Town, The 44–46
Trouble with Harry, The 85–86, 87
True Detective (TV) 63–64
True Grit (2010) 37–39, 59
Twilight Zone, The 111–112

Unforgiven, The 2
Usual Suspects, The 67

VHS 71

Walker Texas Ranger (TV) 34
Walking Dead, The (TV) 3, 15–16, 49, 59, 87
When Harry Met Sally 46–48
Winter's Bone 123–124

For Product Safety Concerns and Information please contact our EU
representative GPSR@taylorandfrancis.com
Taylor & Francis Verlag GmbH, Kaufingerstraße 24, 80331 München, Germany

www.ingramcontent.com/pod-product-compliance
Lightning Source LLC
Chambersburg PA
CBHW070619300426
44113CB00010B/1592